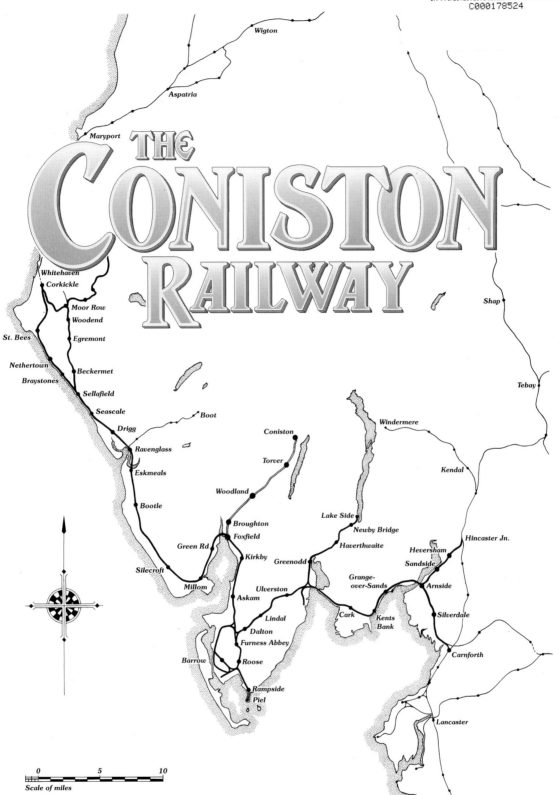

Scale of miles

Michael Andrews and Geoff Holme

**CUMBRIAN
RAILWAYS
ASSOCIATION**

CONTENTS

Front Cover:
Panoramic view of Lake Bank pier, Coniston Lake based on one of the Furness Railway's postcards produced for the Company by Raphael Tuck.
(Geoff Holme collection)

Text © M Andrews, G Holme and the Cumbrian Railways Association 2005
Maps © M Faulkner / M Peascod / A Johnstone and the Cumbrian Railways Association 2005
Photographs © as credited

Published by the Cumbrian Railways Association,
104 Durley Avenue, Pinner, Middlesex HA5 1JH
The Association is a Registered Charity No. 1025436
www.cumbrian-rail.org

Membership Secretary, 36 Clevelands Avenue, Barrow-in-Furness, Cumbria. LA13 0AE

The Association is pleased to acknowledge a generous donation from John Robinson
which has considerably expedited the publication of this book

Design and layout by Alan Johnstone,
24 Hartington Street, Barrow-in-Furness, Cumbria. LA14 5SL
Printed by Lamberts Print & Design, Settle, North Yorkshire

ISBN 0-9540232-3-4

Introduction

The Coniston Railway opened between Broughton and Coniston in 1859, intending to tap the then expanding copper ore traffic from the copper mines at Coniston. To this end the line took a high-level course at Coniston to reach the copper mines wharf, thereby placing the passenger and goods station above the village, and making it accessible only by an inconveniently steep road.

The copper ore traffic soon began to dwindle and by 1890 had ceased, leaving slate, general goods and passengers as the principal traffic, the passengers being mainly tourists in the summer season. The steamer *Gondola*, which the Furness Railway had built and placed on Coniston Lake late in 1859, became one of the principal tourist attractions, so much so that a second steamer *Lady of the Lake* was added in 1908.

This book is a revised and enlarged edition of the Cumbrian Railways Association's first book, originally published in 1985. It tells the story of the planning and building of the Coniston Railway, its late Victorian and Edwardian heyday as a branch of the Furness Railway, and its eventual demise under British Rail ownership as a result of competition from the motor car, the bus and the lorry.

In the text, numbers in [square] brackets indicate the source of the quotation which follows. The key can be found on page 64.

Coniston Station and village. *Situated high above the village, the station, in Paley and Austin's 'Swiss chalet' style of architecture, is seen against the magnificent backdrop of the Above Beck Fells.* (Sankey 6850)

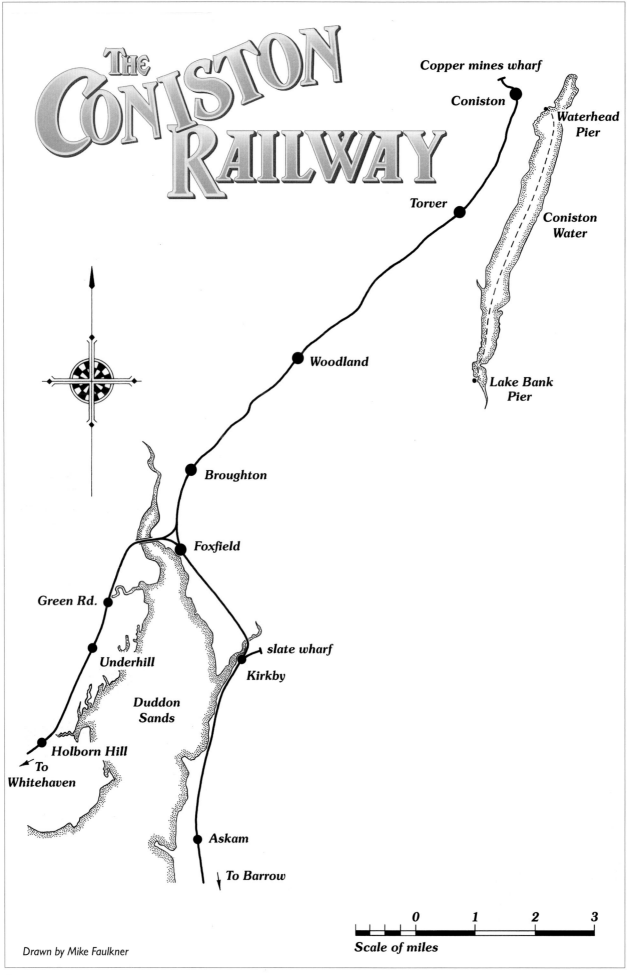

THE CONISTON RAILWAY

Copper mines wharf

Coniston

Waterhead Pier

Torver

Coniston Water

Woodland

Lake Bank Pier

Broughton

Foxfield

Green Rd.

slate wharf

Underhill

Kirkby

Duddon Sands

Holborn Hill

To Whitehaven

Askam

To Barrow

Drawn by Mike Faulkner

0   1   2   3

Scale of miles

These two villages are the principal settlements on the Coniston Railway.

Coniston lies on the west bank of Coniston Lake [1] *nestling in a bosom of rarest beauty*. It is an industrial settlement of great antiquity. Some two thousand years ago the Romans mined here for copper, but the finding of ancient tools suggests that the workings date back to the Bronze Age.

For at least five hundred years Coniston green slate has been extracted, and over the last two hundred years a tourist industry has developed. These industries have all been subject to fluctuations in prosperity. The slate industry was all but wiped out in 1796 when, as a wartime measure, a duty of ten shillings per ton was imposed on slate carried in coastal vessels. It took years for the industry to recover.

Happily, the extraction of Coniston green slate did pick up and continues to be a thriving industry at Brossen Stone Quarry on the face of the 'Old Man' and with limited working of Broughton Moor Quarry near Torver. Both are now managed by the neighbouring Burlington Slate Company at Kirkby, a company still owned by the Cavendish family of Holker Hall, descendants of that 7th Duke of Devonshire who was prominent in the early affairs of the Furness Railway and chairman of the Coniston Railway. While 1960 saw the end of the silver-grey slate production with the closure of the 'Old Man' quarry, 1982 saw extraction of this attractive material start up again when Burlington Slate re-opened Low Brandy Crag Quarry in the Coppermines valley. A further small quarry near Moss Rigg remains privately operated.

Coniston copper ore extraction, records for which go back to Elizabethan times, saw periods of depression, but in 1824 John Taylor took over the Coniston mine. He put in charge John Barratt, who had previously worked with him in Cornwall, and the mine prospered once more. After Taylor withdrew, under Barratt it increased its prosperity. By the mid-1850s it employed some 600 people including many women and children, and produced some 300 tons of ore monthly. Peak production was reached in 1856 when 3,659 tons of ore were produced from workings up to 1,300 feet beneath the surface. After this, decline was rapid. By 1860 production had fallen below 3,000 tons, and only four years later was less than 2,000 tons. This period saw a huge growth in the population of the village, from 480 in 1831 to 1,320 in 1861, most of the influx being miners and their families.

In their heyday the Coniston mines were the largest copper mines in the north of England, finding a ready market in the 18th and early 19th century for copper sheathing for wooden ships. Before the opening of the railway the ore was carried down the lake by boat to Nibthwaite, which became [12]:

> *quite a little lake port for at its landing places*
> *were discharged cargoes of the mineral products*
> *of the Coniston Hills on their way to Ulverston.*

However, by 1877 there was a further decline in the output at Coniston. This was caused by the importation of cheap copper ore from South Africa and Chile, together with the loss of the traditional market as iron replaced wood in shipbuilding and ever more difficult working

Coniston village. *Looking out over the village towards St Andrew's church, with the station signal box prominent in the foreground.*
(Sankey 6851)

General View, Broughton-in-Furness.

Broughton station and village. *The station is seen in its final form after it was extended in 1903.* (Geoff Holme collection)

conditions as the mine workings became deeper. As a result, the mines were abandoned in 1889 [11]. The pumps were stopped in 1897, and so extensive had been the workings that they took five years to flood. The whole mining field is now scheduled as an 'Ancient Industrial Monument', though the dangerous conditions make it essential that visitors do not go underground without an experienced guide.

Amongst other small-scale industries the village has supported over the years was a small iron forge which was started in 1677 using ore imported from Low Furness. The company was taken over by the larger Backbarrow Company in 1712, although iron production continued to about 1757. Before this, much smelting had taken place along the lake when the monks of Furness Abbey preferred to transport iron ore from the Furness area to Coniston rather than transport the fuel to the iron ore.

Other industries included charcoal burning, and this lasted on a large scale until 1920 when the Backbarrow Company converted from charcoal to coke for firing. Final commercial production survived until 1937 when the last gunpowder mill at Gatebeck closed. As with many small industries now long gone, most of the output was for use locally, in the days before the easy transport and mobility enjoyed today wiped out many small concerns.

The tourist industry of Coniston, while of early date, increased in importance in the early years of the 20th century. The railway expanded its programme of tours, which combined road, rail and steamer travel. On some tours, Coniston was used as a base, with coaches taking the participants into the surrounding area. This trade, on which the village now relies more than at any time in its history, has over the years been adversely affected by economic depression and by war, but its most catastrophic experience was the epidemic of foot-and-mouth disease in 2001. The village has a large number of guest houses, ranging from large hotels to one or two rooms in private houses, and is also a base for modern boating activities including boat hire and lake launches.

Coniston is often used as a centre for mountaineering, the walk up to the 'Old Man' being popular from the village. For those wishing for a less strenuous walk, it is possible to get part way up the mountain by road before using the old slate routes to the top, where a magnificent view of the surroundings fells can be obtained. The more adventurous walkers can find more difficult routes, and rock climbers can often be seen on the nearby Dow Crags.

The beauty of the village and its surroundings were appreciated by the Victorians. Notable settlers included the eminent literary figure, John Ruskin, born in 1819, who lived in the village for almost 30 years. He made his home at Brantwood, a decayed country property he had bought in 1871 from the well-known writer and engraver W J Linton for £1,500. Brantwood is on the east side of the lake approximately three miles from the village. It is elevated from the shore and looks over the lake to the 'Old Man'. Since 1951 the house has been owned by the Brantwood Trust, which is part of the Ruskin Foundation set up by Lancaster University. John Ruskin died on 20th January 1900 and is buried in the churchyard at Coniston, his grave being marked by a beautiful green slate cross almost 9 feet in height, made from local stone.

A further memorial in the village is the Ruskin Museum, which in recent years has undergone much development and expansion. It was opened on 31st August 1901 by Canon Rawnsley, one of the founders of the National Trust, and it initially contained the collection of minerals that Ruskin had donated to the Coniston Institute some 16 years earlier. During that time the collection had grown and the new museum included a number of Ruskin's manuscripts, drawings and memorabilia. Major expansion of the museum took place in the late 1990s following a lottery grant and the securing of EU funding. The enlarged museum was officially opened on 23rd May 2000 by Chris Smith, then Secretary of State for Culture, Media and Sport. Today the museum contains a research room and local history library as well as numerous local artefacts. Further expansion is likely to include the remains of the boat *Bluebird* used by Donald Campbell in his water speed record attempts.

Coniston Water is approximately five and a half miles in length and about half a mile in breadth, with a maximum depth of 186 feet. Until pollution from the copper mines all but wiped out the fish, the lake was noted for its char and trout. The stock has been gradually recovering, and licences are issued for limited fishing. No brief history of the village is complete without mention of the lake steamers which the Furness Railway operated, and which are covered in detail in Chapter 8. As well as the rebuilt *Gondola*, other launches run on the lake to Brantwood and Lake Bank, and boats can be hired from the Coniston Boating Centre at Ruskin Pier where the Bluebird Café is situated. This building started life in 1910 as dormitories for Furness Railway staff working on *Gondola* and *Lady of the Lake* which then sailed from Waterhead Pier about 400 yards to the north.

4th January 1967 is a day that will never be forgotten in Coniston history. At 8.55 am Donald Campbell in *Bluebird* was attempting to break the world water speed record. On a calm winter morning, with perfect conditions for record attempts, on his return leg *Bluebird's* bow rose, the craft somersaulted and disappeared from view. At the time of the accident it was estimated he was travelling at around 320 mph. The earlier first leg had been timed at 297 mph, so Campbell was well on course to achieve his dream of a speed record in excess of 300 mph. Campbell was killed instantly and the craft sank in about 150 feet of water, the cause of the accident being the subject of much speculation since. After the wreck was located in August 2000, it was inevitable that attempts would be made to raise it, and these were completed on 8th March 2001 when she was lifted out of the lake at the Bluebird Café. Shortly afterwards Campbell's body was discovered, and on 28th May it was raised and brought ashore at Pier Cottage where he had left on his record attempt over 34 years earlier. After confirmation of identity, a funeral was held on 12th September 2001 at St. Andrew's church, after which he was laid to rest in the cemetery in Hawkshead Old Road.

Coniston was considered, by mid-18th century standards, to be adequately served by roads. It was situated on the Ambleside to Broughton road (now A593) but it should be noted that, in order to attract the Coniston copper ore to their terminus at Broughton, the Furness Railway Company had, in 1849, to expend £500 on the improvement of this road. The road to Greenodd (now A5084) was described as [6] *excellent*, and was used between Nibthwaite and Greenodd by the copper traffic until this was transferred to the railway at Coniston in 1860. John Ruskin in a letter to the Ulverston Mirror of 5th September 1874 bemoaned the railway taking the long route via Broughton, which resulted from the early railway geography and a requirement

Coniston station and village, *c.1905-8. The view from the tower of St Andrew's church, looking towards the station.*
(Sankey 2777)

Broughton Square, *c.1928. The square is dominated by an obelisk. Beside it, awaiting its next turn of duty, is a bus belonging to Creighton Motors, one of the many small local bus operators competing for business in the late 1920s.* *(Lance Kelly collection)*

for a railway for minerals rather than for the tourist trade on which it later came to rely:

> The town of Ulverston is twelve miles from me, by four miles of mountain road by Coniston Lake, three through a pastoral valley and five by the sea side. A healthier or lovelier walk would be difficult to find. But now the traveller would never think of doing such a thing. He first walks three miles in a contrary direction to a railroad station and then travels by railroad twenty-four miles to Ulverston paying two shillings fare. During the twenty-four miles transit he is idle, dusty, stupid and either more or less cold than is pleasant to him. In either case he drinks beer at two or three stations and passes his time between them with anyone he can find, in talking without having anything to talk about, and such talk always becomes vicious, he arrives at Ulverston jaded, half drunk and otherwise demoralised and three shillings at least the poorer than in the morning.

The township of Broughton had a similar population to Coniston, the 1871 census showing Coniston with 1,106 and Broughton with 1,255 inhabitants. However, the two places were significantly different. Broughton had no heavy industry; the cottage industry of wool spinning was wiped out by the mechanisation of this activity leaving swill-making and the traditional trades of the black-smith, the carpenter and the other activities needed by an agricultural community.

As at Coniston, the Lords of the Manor of Broughton dated back to the Norman Conquest, but, unlike at Coniston where the le Flemings were still in office at the time of the Coniston Railway Act of 1857, the Broughtons had long been extinguished. They had built the piel tower in 1314 to defend themselves against marauding Scots, and Broughton Tower, rebuilt and extended and now converted into luxury flats, survives to this day. They were supporters of the Yorkist cause in the Wars of the Roses and, undeterred by their defeat at Bosworth in 1485, they gave support to the Plantagenet pretender Lambert Simnel when he landed with an army at Piel Harbour near Barrow in 1487. The defeat of this army by the forces of Henry VII at Stoke led to the attainder of Sir Thomas Broughton, and his estates were given to the Stanleys, Earls of Derby. The Stanleys supported the Royalist side in the Civil War with fatal results. The Crown awarded the Broughton estates to the Sawreys in 1658, who remained Lords of the Manor of Broughton until recent times when this right passed to Lancashire, and later Cumbria, County Council. As Lords of the Manor the County Council is now responsible for reading out the Broughton Charter in the square on 1st August each year and for the traditional distribution of pennies to the local children.

A notable event in the development of Broughton was the building of the Square and Town Hall by John Gilpin Sawrey in 1760. Until the mid-19th century Broughton had a Friday Market, but this was abandoned once the market at Ulverston could be reached by Furness Railway trains.

Older generations of rail travellers may remember the Coniston branch as a modest single line from Foxfield operated by a push-and-pull motor train consisting of ancient stock hauled by an even more ancient tank locomotive. Fell walkers would purchase a workman's return from Barrow Central to Coniston as the first leg of a hike to Coniston Old Man, or, if they were more ambitious, to Scafell Pike, the highest mountain in England. The Coniston branch had, however, a more complex and interesting history than these latter-day travellers would imagine.

On 3rd June 1846, some two years after its Incorporation, the Furness Railway Company opened its main line for goods and mineral traffic from Crooklands to Barrow, together with a branch from Millwood Junction, near Dalton, to a slate wharf near Kirkby. The Kirkby Slate Quarries were owned by William Cavendish, Earl of Burlington, and his interest in these quarries had been one of the prime factors in the conception of the Furness Railway.

The extension of the Furness Railway eastward beyond Dalton had been fraught with difficulty. It had been the original intention to build the line to Ulverston and, in the 'Railway Mania' year of 1845, there were no less than three different schemes to continue a line of railway east to connect with the Lancaster & Carlisle and 'Little' North Western systems. Such lines would have afforded access to Coniston by way of a branch along the Crake Valley,

but all three schemes failed and the post-mania depression in railway promotion set in.

In 1845 during the construction of its original line, the Furness Railway had instructed their engineer, J R McClean, to carry out preliminary surveys for extensions of their line, and one such survey was between Kirkby and Coniston Waterhead. However, only the extension from Crooklands to Ulverston and Kirkby to Broughton were proceeded with, being authorised by the Furness Railway Act 1846.

By the time the Broughton extension was opened in February 1848, the Whitehaven & Furness Junction Railway, authorised in 1845, was finding itself short of capital. Consequently, it was obliged to divert its proposed line over the direct Duddon Crossing, which would have joined the Furness Railway near Ireleth, to a less-expensive alternative line through Underhill to join the Furness extension near Foxfield.

Coniston at this time presented an attraction to railway promoters because of the proximity of the copper mines. While being of great antiquity, they were approaching the zenith of their output, and produced, in 1855, 300 tons of copper ore per month. In addition there was a growing tourist trade in the Lake District. As early as August 1846, the Furness Railway had arranged for conveyances to run between Kirkby station and Coniston. On 12th December 1848 the Furness Railway Board agreed to carry copper ore for no more than 3s. 6d. ($17^1/_2$ p) per ton and to spend £500 on the improvement of the road between

Copper House and Wharf, c.1962. Used originally to load copper ore and later slate onto wagons for transport along the branch. By this date the buildings were being used by other light industries. Equipment for making concrete blocks can be seen in the centre of the picture.   *(Michael Andrews MAA 136.1)*

Broughton and Coniston. On 1st November 1850, the Whitehaven & Furness Junction Railway opened the last section of their line to a junction with the Furness Railway near Foxfield, and obtained running rights over the Furness line to Broughton for £150 per annum. Broughton in Furness thus became the terminus of the two railways.

In 1850 there was little prospect of either the Furness or the Whitehaven & Furness companies achieving their ambition of a rail link across the county to the Lancaster & Carlisle Railway in the Carnforth area. Northwards they depended on the Whitehaven & Furness Junction's link across Whitehaven via a street tramway to its northern neighbour, the Whitehaven Junction Railway. Otherwise there was a steamer link across Morecambe Bay to Fleetwood from the privately owned pier at Piel. Although the Bill for the Ulverstone & Lancaster Railway was in preparation, the project would obviously take several years to complete. For a rail route to Coniston, that from Broughton was the only practical one at this time.

W B Kendall, the Furness Railway's first historian, records that in 1849 John Barraclough Fell, the Furness contractor, was planning a narrow-gauge railway to Coniston to tap the copper and slate traffic [7]. Lord Burlington of Holker Hall, Cartmel, then Furness Railway chairman, noted in his diary on 8th November 1849:

> I came home by Mr Fell's and found Mr Ramsden [the Furness Railway manager] there. Mr Stileman [of McClean and Stileman, Furness Railway engineers] had been down to look at his [Fell's] proposed Coniston Railway. It seems altogether a desirable undertaking, but I fear it will not go ahead for want of funds.

This plan indeed did not come to fruition, and it was not until 1857 that the nominally independent Coniston Railway Company was authorised to build a standard gauge line from Broughton to Coniston.

The Coniston Railway Act received Royal Assent on 10th August 1857, but the independence was no more than a manoeuvre to raise risk capital from the copper mine owners and lessees at a low rate of interest. Of the £45,000 capital, £20,000 was to be subscribed by Lady le Fleming, Lord of the Manor of Coniston, and John Barratt, James Humbleton and Joseph Mason, lessees of the mines, at a fixed initial dividend of 2%.

Coniston signal box and shed, *c.1947. The south end of the station site, with freight being shunted in the foreground. Coniston Water can be seen in the distance.*
(John Hext collection)

On 27th August 1857, shortly after the passing of the Coniston Railway Act, a shareholders' meeting was held at the Waterhead Inn, Coniston. Those present, according to the Minute Book, were Lord Burlington, Messrs. Nicholl and Eddy (all Furness Railway Directors), James Ramsden (the Furness Railway Secretary and Manager) and J R McClean (the Furness Railway Consulting Engineer). The meeting closed, to re-open as a Directors' Meeting, at which Ramsden was appointed Secretary and the civil engineering partnership of McClean and Stileman as Engineers. Thereafter the Coniston Railway meetings were in fact no more than appendices to the meetings of the Furness Railway Directors and Shareholders.

On 7th November 1857, at 9 Burlington Street, London, the Directors considered tenders for the construction of the line. The Engineer's estimated cost was £23,370, and the contract was awarded to Child & Pickles for £20,907, for completion by March 1859. The contractors, for reasons which are not clear, ran into difficulties and became bankrupt in August 1858. The Furness Railway then took over responsibility for the works. The contractors who had just completed work on the Furness Railway at Millwood and Foxfield, Gradwell & Gumley, appear to have been given work on the line.

Difficulties had already arisen in Broughton where two roads were to be crossed by the new line. Certain local residents objected to the proposed level crossing, while others were concerned that a bridge was unrealistic and would cause the destruction of property in the town. Lt. Col. Yolland, an Inspecting Officer from the Railway Department of the Board of Trade, was sent down to investigate, and in his report on 14th April 1858 strongly supported the level crossing as authorised in the Act.

Col. Yolland inspected the railway throughout on 25th May 1859, noting the soundness of the permanent way and civil engineering structures, but recommending improvements to the signalling arrangements. At Broughton a distant signal was required on the approach from Foxfield, and the levers for working the signals needed to be brought together onto the platform. Station buildings at Woodland and Coniston had only just been commenced. Signal arrangements at Woodland, Torver and Coniston were not only incomplete but the distants again needed moving further out. There was no turntable at Coniston. In this state of incompleteness he could not sanction the opening of the line.

On 14th June 1859, Col. Yolland was back again. This time he noted that temporary buildings had been provided and that signalling was complete. He had also received an undertaking from the Duke of Devonshire, formerly the Earl of Burlington, that the three sections of the line would be worked by one train only, and that tank engines would be used on the line pending the construction of turntables. He recommended the approval of the opening of the line subject to the removal of points facing into a ballast pit.

The line was opened for passenger traffic on 18th June 1859, although the final section from Coniston station to the Coppermines Wharf did not come into use until 1860. The Duke of Devonshire noted in his diary on 8th February 1860:

> We went to Coniston and had a meeting with
> Mr Barratt to make arrangements respecting
> copper ore about which he had been rather
> troublesome.

In the meantime events of greater moment had been taking place. In 1851 the Ulverstone & Lancaster Railway had been authorised. Construction was beset with difficulties, both technical and financial, but the line was eventually opened between Carnforth and Ulverston in 1857. To the north, the Whitehaven Tunnel connecting the Whitehaven & Furness and Whitehaven Junction lines had been opened in 1852, creating a through route between Carlisle and Barrow. In 1854 the Whitehaven, Cleator & Egremont Railway had been authorised to connect the iron ore mines around Cleator with the Whitehaven & Furness Junction line at Mirehouse, south of Whitehaven. In consequence of all these developments, high hopes were entertained for the Whitehaven to Carnforth through route as a means of opening up the West Cumberland iron ore field.

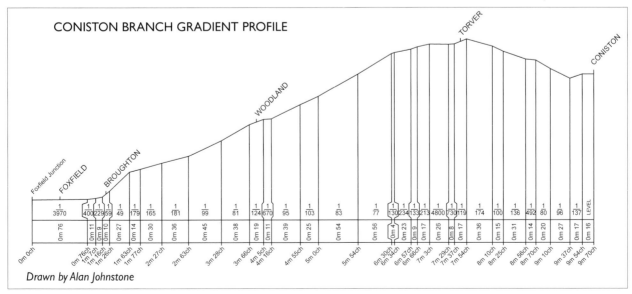

Drawn by Alan Johnstone

Five Arches Viaduct. *The largest structure on the line was a 5-arch bridge about a mile and a half south of Woodland Station. It crossed a minor road and a ravine, and survived until demolition in the mid-1980s.* (Lance Kelly collection)

It had, however, the disadvantage of reversals at Broughton and at Millwood, north of Barrow, and consequently plans were made for the building of 'expedition curves' at Foxfield and Millwood.

The two curves were opened for traffic on 1st August 1858, and from this date the junction for Broughton, and soon Coniston, became Foxfield, where a joint Whitehaven & Furness and Furness engine shed and sidings were constructed. By an agreement of 1st January 1861 the joint use of the Foxfield and Broughton stations was continued, though the original direct line from the Whitehaven & Furness towards Broughton fell into disuse and was subsequently lifted. The Coniston Railway Company was amalgamated with the Furness Railway in 1862.

One final political drama which might have affected the Coniston branch remained to be played out. By 1864, after many years of penury, the Whitehaven & Furness Junction Railway was becoming profitable, largely as a result of the traffic received from the Whitehaven, Cleator & Egremont Railway. The two companies were authorised to build a joint line from Egremont to Sellafield, providing a more direct route for southbound ore traffic. The Whitehaven & Furness, in an attempt to improve its route south, resurrected its original proposal for a line across the Duddon Estuary, adding a further link from Ireleth to Ulverston. This would mirror the Solway Junction scheme to shorten the route north from West Cumberland to the iron furnaces of Lanarkshire. The response of the Furness Railway was to propose its own line across the Duddon – straight into its new docks then under construction at Barrow.

These schemes came before Parliament in 1865, in what proved to be a fateful session. The Furness was inextricably involved in the ambitions of both the LNWR and the Midland companies. While the Midland was committed to the Furness & Midland Joint Line from Wennington to Carnforth, and also looked towards Carlisle and Scotland, the LNWR was poised to strike into West Cumberland. The Parliamentary Committee approved the Whitehaven & Furness Duddon crossing scheme and rejected that of the Furness. Within a few weeks the LNWR had agreed to take over the Whitehaven Junction and Cockermouth & Workington Railways, and Furness the Whitehaven & Furness Junction. So from 1866 the Furness system had been extended to Whitehaven and the company was committed to building the Duddon crossing they had opposed. As this project involved the abandonment of the line between Millom and Foxfield, the junction for the Coniston branch would have been brought as far south as Askam. However, the depression in trade from 1866 led to a reappraisal of the Duddon crossing and, despite opposition, an Act to abandon it was obtained in 1869.

Foxfield

The Coniston Railway properly began at Broughton, but very soon the junction shifted to the little hamlet of Foxfield on the edge of the Duddon Estuary. From its opening, the line was worked by the Furness Railway, and from a practical point of view formed part of that company's system. The first plans for a station at Foxfield appeared in 1857. This was in connection with the proposed 'Foxfield South Fork' line to allow direct running between Whitehaven and Carnforth. A plan of that year shows an island platform, an engine shed and turntable for the Whitehaven & Furness Company, and a station house on the adjacent public road.

Capt. George Ross of the Railway Department inspected the new curve and station in July 1858. The signalling was incomplete and obliged him to return later to make a further inspection. The turntable was still not finished, and he required that locomotives be turned on the triangle formed by the old and new lines. The turntable was soon completed and the old line fell into disuse. It was subsequently taken up, although its course can still be seen: at the east end of the cutting leading towards the viaduct, the trackbed widens out for the former junction of the direct line to Broughton, and this joined the Furness line from Foxfield opposite Sandgap Farm. Foxfield joint station was opened on 1st August 1858.

The original island platform was only 13 feet 6 inches wide and the west face was enclosed within a small passenger shed 100 feet in length. A canopy supported by four columns protected southbound passengers. On the seaward side of the passenger shed was a smaller goods shed 70 feet in length. A miniscule booking office was provided at the north end of the platform.

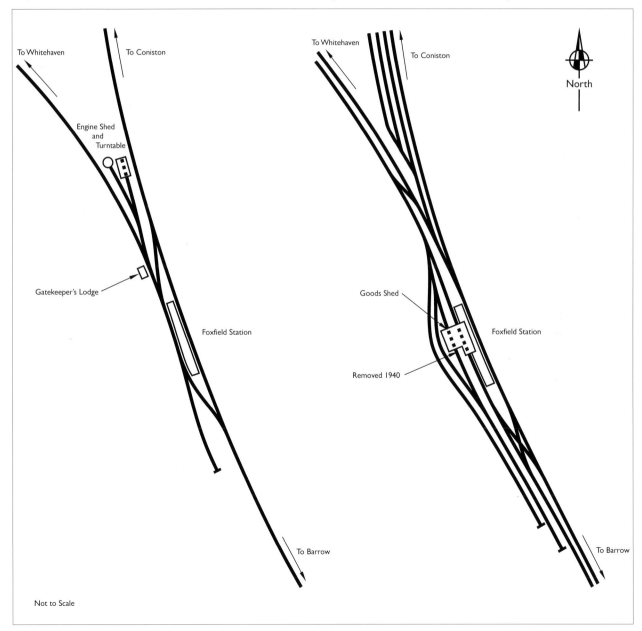

To Whitehaven · To Coniston

Engine Shed and Turntable

Gatekeeper's Lodge

Foxfield Station

To Barrow

Not to Scale

To Whitehaven · To Coniston

North

Goods Shed

Foxfield Station

Removed 1940

To Barrow

The development of Foxfield station. On the left is shown the track formation of August 1858, when Foxfield became the junction for the main line to Whitehaven and the branch line to Coniston. On the right is shown the final development with sidings and goods shed.
(Mike Faulkner/Mike Peascod, based on plans at Barrow Record Office)

Prior to the rebuilding of this station in 1879 there were two abortive plans for an enlarged station at Foxfield. In June 1863 the directors of the Whitehaven & Furness Junction Railway, whose line was now beginning to show a good profit, approved plans for a new joint station at Foxfield. However, it was soon after this that they decided to resurrect the Duddon crossing proposals as originally authorised in 1845, and the station plan was soon forgotten.

A second plan for an enlarged station at Foxfield was produced by the Furness Railway in 1873. This involved an extension of the island platform, enlarged station buildings, and up and down goods loops and yards. This plan came at a time when the Furness Railway was planning a new main line between Lindal and Park by way of Gleaston, Salthouse, the Barrow loop and Ormsgill. After 1873 a long depression in trade set in and only the line between Salthouse and Park via Barrow Central station was in fact built, being opened in 1882.

The architects Paley & Austin produced plans for an enlarged station at Foxfield in 1877, and this final Foxfield station was completed by the Barrow contractor, William Ormandy, in 1879. The island platform was widened to 29 feet, a new canopy with seven columns provided and the arches of the passenger shed widened. New buildings were constructed at each end of the passenger shed.

In 1909, a facing crossover was provided in the down main line south of the station to allow direct running onto the branch. After this, the station survived in this form until the closure of the branch, when it lost its status as a junction.

Foxfield station, c.1908. A view from inside the passenger shed on the northbound platform. The arch in the north wall replaced a stone round-top arch which was only a little wider than the trains. In the background is the engine shed constructed for the Whitehaven & Furness Junction Railway. It survived in alternative use until the mid-1970s. (W Pinch collection)

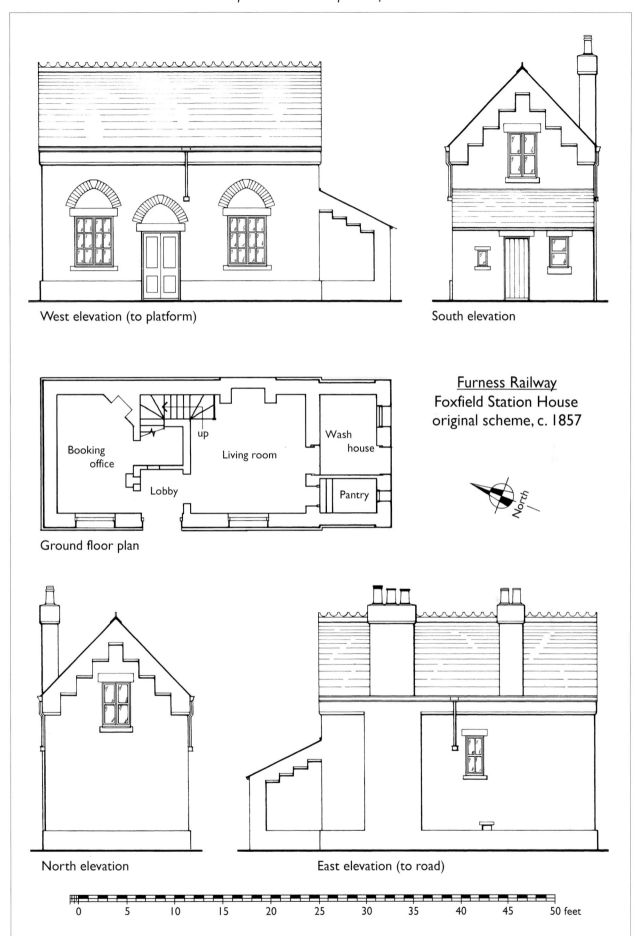

West elevation (to platform)

South elevation

Booking office

Lobby

up

Living room

Wash house

Pantry

Ground floor plan

Furness Railway
Foxfield Station House
original scheme, c. 1857

North

North elevation

East elevation (to road)

0   5   10   15   20   25   30   35   40   45   50 feet

Foxfield Station House, *c.1858. The building served both as station offices and the stationmaster's house, and survives, with extensions, as a private residence.*   *(Mike Faulkner, based on plans at Barrow Record Office)*

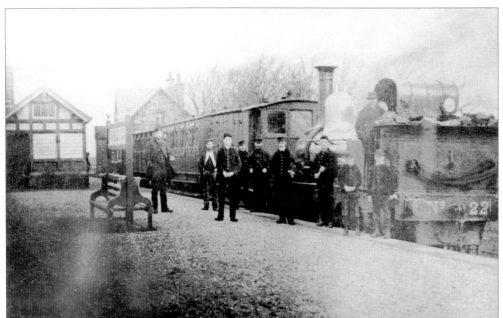

Foxfield station,
c.1886. 2-2-2WT No.
22, one of the early
passenger engines to be
used on the branch, is on
a Coniston to Foxfield
branch train.
(Ken Norman collection)

Foxfield station Up
platform, c.1907.
Looking northwards
along the island platform,
the typical Paley and
Austin timber and stone
construction of the 1879
buildings can be seen.
The signal box is at the
far end of the platform,
with its raised platform
to facilitate handling the
token for the Foxfield-
Broughton section of the
branch. On the right is
the Station House, in
front of which are posed
the station staff with
their stationmaster,
J W Irving.
(Geoff Holme collection)

Foxfield,
18th September 1951.
Class 5 4-6-0 No. 44950
is coming off the branch
with the 5.40 pm
Coniston to Blackpool
working.
(Alan Pearsall C69)

Broughton

The original line from Kirkby-in-Furness to Broughton had been constructed under powers obtained by the Furness Railway Extension Act of 1846. The single line was inspected by Capt. Simmons of the Railway Inspectorate on 23rd February 1848 and approved for passenger traffic.

From 1850 the station at Broughton became joint with the Whitehaven & Furness company, and a plan of that date shows a platform for the joint use of both companies. The Whitehaven & Furness had use of an engine shed, while the Furness Railway had a goods shed, turntable and sidings, all on the site which later became the goods yard. A booking office similar to that at Foxfield was built at the south end of Old Street. The extension of the railway to Coniston, on a rising grade of 1 in 59, swept away the engine shed and the passenger platform. New station buildings, later to be extended, were built on the new platform, which was on the west side of the line to Coniston. Two roads were closed and a level crossing provided over the Ulverston Road, at which point the line was rising at 1 in 49.

After the opening to Coniston in 1859, Broughton station seems to have remained undisturbed until the implications of the Regulation of Railways Act of 1889 were

felt. Prior to the introduction of Electric Train Tablet working between Foxfield and Coniston on 31st May 1897, a new signal box and signalling were provided. However, Col. Yorke, in the course of his inspection, took exception to the shunting of passenger trains into the goods yard to allow trains to cross at Broughton. He required that a new loop and platform be provided, works which were not completed until 8th July 1903.

The final inspection of the new loop and platform by Major Druitt yielded the following example of contemporary Civil Service literary style:

> Owing to the levels of the ground at this station it was impossible without great expense to place the platforms opposite each other and in order to enable trains to pass each other while standing in either platform it is necessary for the up trains to use the usual down loop line and vice versa, as the platform on the proper up side is at the down end of the platform on the proper down side. I see no objection to this unusual arrangement which was approved by the Board of Trade provisionally.

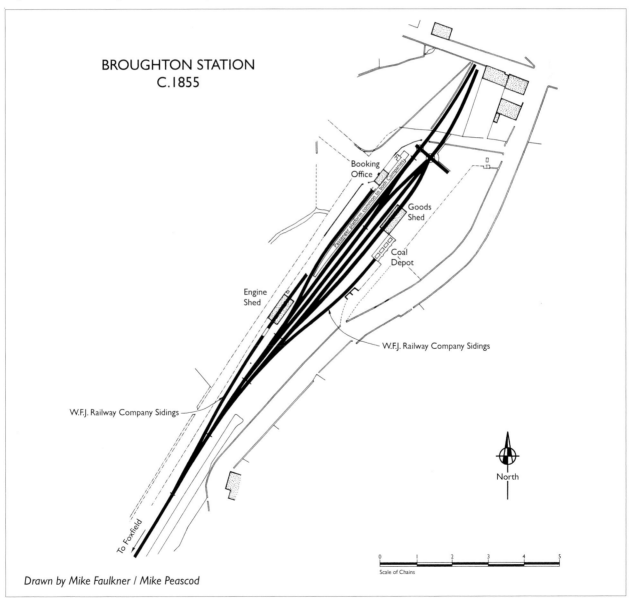

Drawn by Mike Faulkner / Mike Peascod

Broughton station, *c.1907. The Furness Railway railmotor is arriving. The passing loop of 1903 can be seen diverging in the foreground.* *(Geoff Holme collection)*

Broughton station, *August 1958. Taken shortly before closure, showing the main station building in its final form. At the time the alterations to the track layout were taking place, the stationmaster's house was extended. An undated plan shows the addition of a bedroom above the former enclosed yard at the right hand side of this building, costing the then considerable sum of £42.* *(CRA Alan Headech collection HEA 065)*

Broughton signal box, *c.1958. The signal box, built when the branch re-signalling took place in 1896, is seen here standing guard over the gated level crossing provided on the road to Dalton and Barrow.   (Michael Andrews MAA 126)*

Broughton goods yard, *24th August 1957. Broughton was provided with a large goods yard when it was the terminus of the lines from both Barrow and Whitehaven, and the layout survived basically intact until closure of the branch. On the extreme right is the ground frame provided to control the entrance to the yard from the 1903 passenger loop.   (Alan Pearsall J922)*

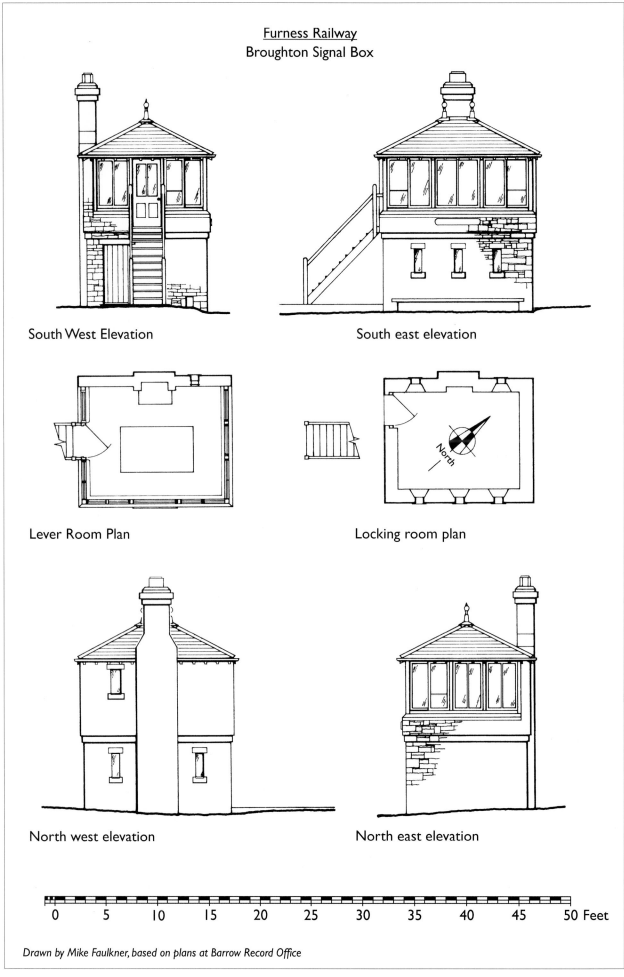

Furness Railway
Broughton Signal Box

South West Elevation

South east elevation

Lever Room Plan

Locking room plan

North west elevation

North east elevation

0   5   10   15   20   25   30   35   40   45   50 Feet

Drawn by Mike Faulkner, based on plans at Barrow Record Office

Woodland

From Broughton station the Coniston branch climbed at 1 in 49 through a cutting on the south-east border of the Broughton Tower Estate and continued its upward grade for the 2¹/₂ miles to Woodland. This station was built in an idyllic setting perched on the side of a hill overlooking the scattered farms, fields and rocky outcrops of that wildest part of High Furness, Subberthwaite. The commercial justification for a station in this place remains a matter for speculation. This location did, however, provide the opportunity to make a passing place. As originally built, this station had one platform on the down side and a short loop and siding. However, in connection with the improvements prior to the introduction of Electric Train

Tablet working in 1897, an up loop, platform and waiting room, together with a signal box were provided. Work on these alterations did not start until well into 1896. The signal box plans state that it was to be built before the waiting shed on the new up platform. This makes it highly likely that the waiting shed was not ready when the new platform came into use. While both shelter and signal box were mainly of timber construction, the latter would be mounted on a Coniston stone base forming the locking room, with a concrete floor 12 inches below rail level. The waiting shelter was estimated to cost £50. Construction details for both buildings appear on a Furness Railway drawing dated 18th May 1896.

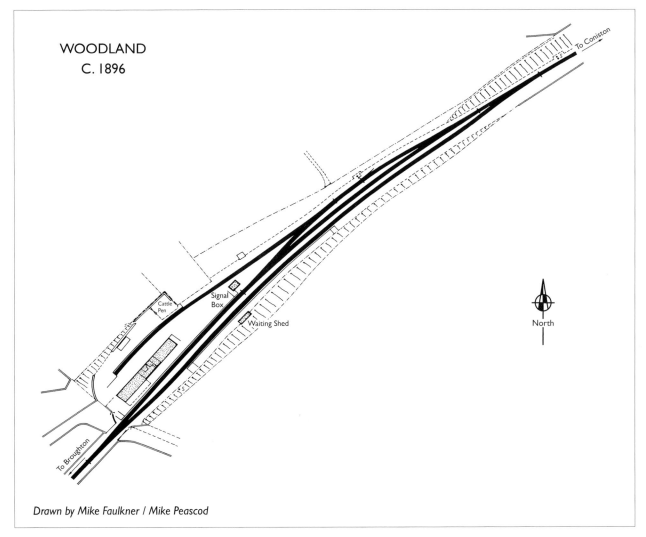

WOODLAND
C. 1896

Drawn by Mike Faulkner / Mike Peascod

Woodland station, *c.1956. The branch push-pull train is ready to depart for Foxfield, with the locomotive in the 'push' position at the far end of the train.* *(J Martin Hurst, Ken Norman collection HNA 2)*

Woodland station and signal box, *1961. One of the thrice-weekly freight services, hauled by 0-6-0T No. 47531, is passing through the closed station at Woodland on its way to Coniston. The signal box was retained to allow access to the siding behind it.* *(Michael Andrews MAA 127)*

Woodland station. *Rebuilt Sharp, Stewart 0-6-0 locomotive No. 88 is seen hauling a branch freight train which includes an early container on a flat wagon. Travelling light towards Coniston tender first, 4-4-0 locomotive No. 125 is in the down platform.*

(Ken Norman collection KNO 834)

Woodland station and level crossing, *April 1962. In the final week of operation, the freight service is seen on the approach to Woodland, waiting for the crossing gates to be opened to allow it to continue to Coniston.* *(John Hext collection)*

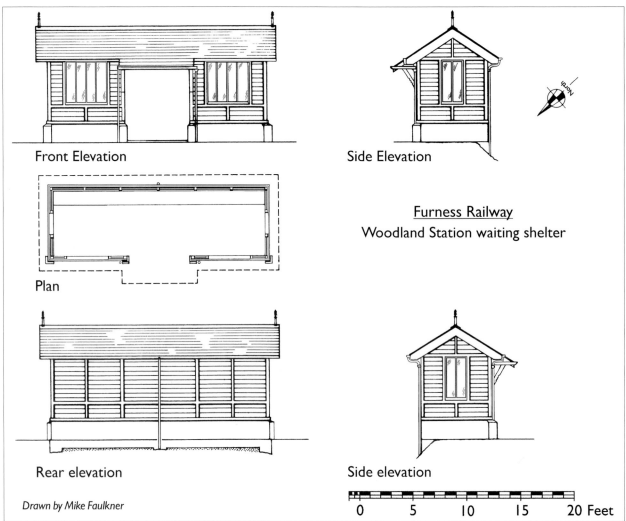

Front Elevation

Side Elevation

Plan

Furness Railway
Woodland Station waiting shelter

Rear elevation

Side elevation

Drawn by Mike Faulkner

0   5   10   15   20 Feet

Woodland Station.

Woodland station, *c.1905. The station buildings here also served the local community as a Post Office complete with separate entrance at the south end of the platform. The gates are closed to road traffic, and the station staff pose on the platform. (Geoff Holme collection)*

Torver

The summit of the Coniston branch was reached about half a mile short of Torver near the Dalton Road level crossing. Torver, like Woodland, had one platform on the down side but a passing loop and goods yard were on the up side. The station was handy for the nearby church and the Church House Inn, the latter institution tending to be the more popular with travellers. Cottages were built by the Furness Railway at Torver in 1867. As at the other stations on the line, alterations were carried out prior to the introduction of Electric Train Tablet working in 1897 and Torver ceased to be a block post and passing place. The loop and the old disc signals were removed and the connection into the goods yard was operated by a two-lever ground frame controlled by the tablet.

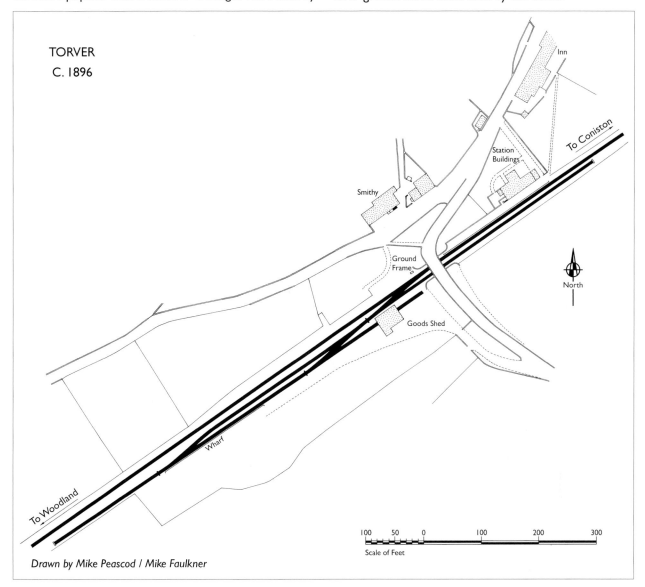

TORVER
C. 1896

Drawn by Mike Peascod / Mike Faulkner

Torver station, *c.1910. The long siding here served as a headshunt for the goods yard on the far side of the bridge. The bridge has long been demolished, but the house and station buildings survive in private ownership.* *(Geoff Roe collection)*

Torver goods shed, *c.1958. Built in local slate to a standard design, but with an additional office at the rear. Access to the yard and shed was by a ground frame near the bridge, which was locked by the train tablet to prevent unauthorised movements of the points.* *(CRA Alan Headech collection HEA 084)*

Torver station, *c.1908. The station staff are ready to meet the branch train from Coniston, headed by one of the 0-6-2 tank engines often used on the branch services.* *(Lance Kelly collection)*

Dalton Road Gates, *c.1935. A crossing and a crossing keeper's cottage were provided about half a mile south of Torver. While the railway has gone, the cottage still survives, but instead of trains, road traffic now passes by, as the track bed north from the cottage to Torver has been incorporated into improvements to the A593 road.* *(CRA Pattinson collection PA 0247)*

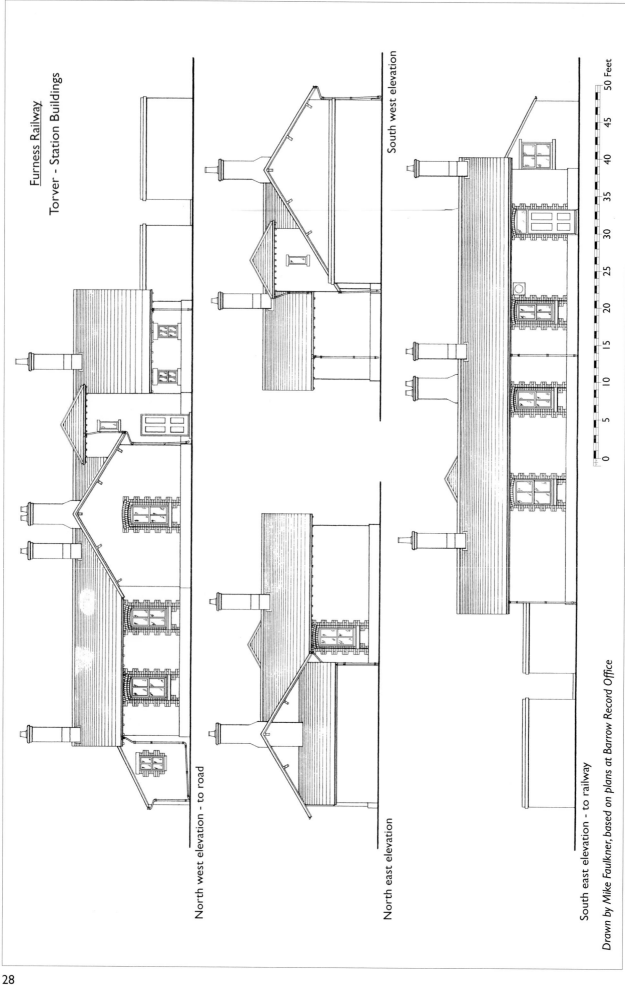

Furness Railway
Torver - Station Buildings

South west elevation

North west elevation - to road

North east elevation

South east elevation - to railway

Drawn by Mike Faulkner, based on plans at Barrow Record Office

0 5 10 15 20 25 30 35 40 45 50 Feet

Coniston

From Torver the Coniston branch continued on a mainly falling gradient through Park Gate level crossing to reach the passenger terminus at Coniston station, the high level inconveniently above the village being needed to access the copper mines wharf. No details have survived of the original buildings, but in 1862, Edward Paley of Lancaster, the consulting architect to the Furness Railway, provided plans for a station at Coniston. An early

photograph of FR 2-2-2 well tank No. 37 at the head of an up train, reproduced on page 48, shows this station before any southern extensions to the original building had been built.

Originally there was only one through platform, this being the line which led to the copper mines wharf further up the valley. The second line which entered the train shed terminated at a stop block shortly before

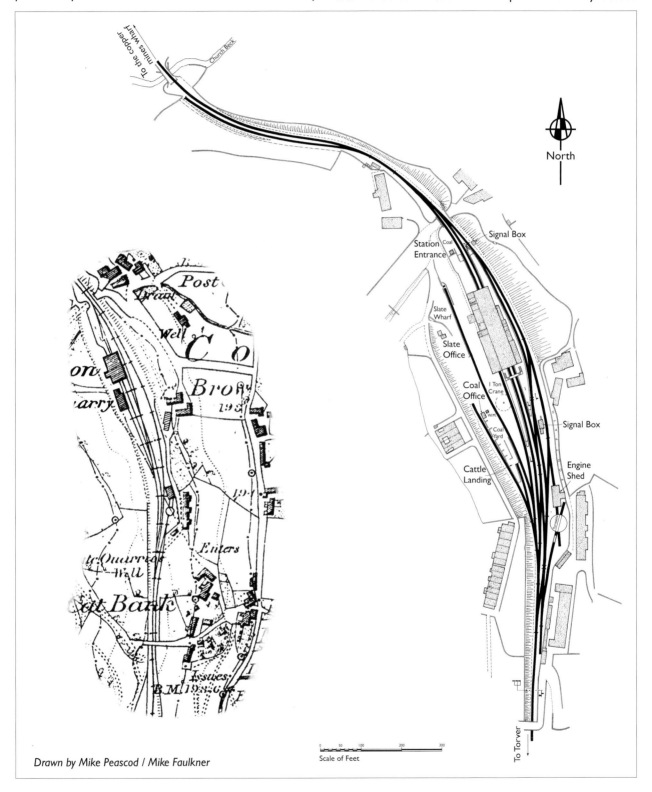

Drawn by Mike Peascod / Mike Faulkner

Scale of Feet

Coniston station. *Inset shows an early layout at Coniston, expanded to include a through road and a bay road under an overall roof, together with a small yard. The main drawing shows the final layout of 1896, at the time when the branch was re-signalled.*

reaching the northern glazed screen. In 1888 the enlargement of Coniston Station was charged to Capital Accounts and similar charges recurred over a ten-year period. Most of the work was complete by the end of 1892 at a cost of over £4,000. The train shed was approximately doubled in length, and the goods shed was also enlarged. In the extensions were included the ventilation tower for the gents lavatory and all the building south of this point. On completion, a wood and glass screen similar in style to the one then existing at the north end was provided. At the north end the original screen was not wide enough for two platforms and double track. When a second platform was provided and the track extended to form a through road, this screen had to be removed. In its place a wider archway made from old sections of rail was provided, which was then filled in with the wood and glass screen which can be seen on photographs of this end of the station. The station many readers will remember was completed by the addition of the third platform and waiting shelter together with additional facilities in 1896 at a further cost of £750. As a result of its severe curve, this third platform was not favoured by the operators and did not see a great deal of use.

A plan of Coniston dated 7th May 1897 was submitted to the Board of Trade and showed the addition of the No. 3 Platform, extensions of Platforms Nos. 1 and 2, a new signalbox and a complete re-signalling in accordance with the 1889 Regulation of Railways Act's requirements. The north end of the station was worked from a 15-lever ground frame. From the station the single line to the Coppermines Wharf disappeared out of sight on a left-hand curve. Some time before World War 1 the Coal Siding was removed from the northern end of the station to its position at the southern edge of the site shown in the main plan.

As at many other stations where visitors would stop on their tours, the Furness Railway provided a refreshment room at Coniston. This was built at a cost of £376, including moving the carriage dock to another site, and is shown as complete on 17th June 1905 in the Engineers cost book. When the board authorised this structure they were expecting an improvement on the 10,816 tourists that had passed though the station during the 1904 season. A plan dated 3rd January 1906 shows a 54ft x 18ft wooden extension, together with a yard on the north end of the Platform 1, containing a kitchen, larder and tea room with 17 tables. Like the rest of the Furness Railway catering, this was let to Spiers and Pond of London, who charged from 6d. (2.5p) to 1s. 6d. (7.5p) for lunch or tea. The room was removed shortly after World War 1.

Mention must be made of the little stone engine shed on its very cramped site, which was used to stable the branch engine overnight. Originally the only access was via the turntable, but this was obviously not possible for the larger locomotives. After a fire in the early days of World War II, the shed was rebuilt with a new flat roof. It made the shed a safer working environment, even if it did little to improve its appearance.

The Furness Railway also built the road up to the station. This was a steep climb which must have taxed humans and horses alike until the advent of the motorised era between the two world wars.

Coniston station. *The station is seen in its superb setting overlooking the lake and the village. In this 1930s view the station has reached its full development and the competition by road has yet to affect the varied wagon load freight around the yard.*

(W Potter, Ken Norman collection KNQ 434)

Station porch, *(above) c.1958. Shortly before closure, the station porch and buildings are seen from the approach road. The northern end of this building housed the Refreshment Room.* ***Station weather-vane,*** *(inset) c.1958. Situated above the porch to the original 1859 station, this attractive weather-vane survived the numerous alterations to the station building.* *(Bob Davey, Derek Brough)*

Blackpool through train, *18th September 1951. For some years after the end of World War II, a train ran twice a week from Blackpool to Coniston. Here the train is seen ready to depart at 5.40 pm for the return journey to Blackpool.* *(Alan Pearsall C64)*

Coniston station, c.1893. 2-4-2 tank locomotive No. 73 with a train at the original through platform, and showing the wood and glazed screen at the north end before its replacement. (John Hext collection)

Coniston station, c.1947. An ex-L&Y 2-4-2 tank is seen here at the head of the push-pull train from Foxfield at the north end of the station. (John Hext collection)

Coniston station, c.1958. Ivatt 2-6-2 tank 41217 is seen here at the head of the branch train from Foxfield. These modern locomotives were kept at Barrow for use on the branch for the final years of its existence, and were transferred away immediately after closure. (John Hext collection)

Coniston engine shed, *c.1947. Coniston shed was a sub-shed of Barrow for many years until closure. Here on the trip train from Barrow Yard is an ex-LNWR 0-6-0 Coal Engine. In this typical scene from a branch line shed, notice the large heaps, cinders from the fireboxes and smoke boxes of the engines using the shed.*

(John Hext)

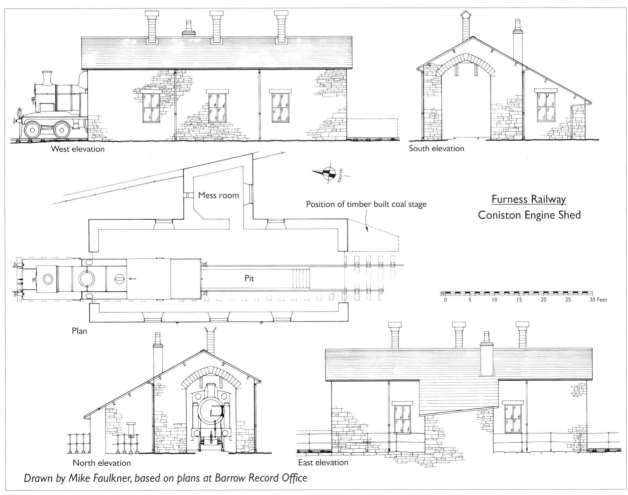

West elevation

South elevation

Mess room

North

Position of timber built coal stage

Pit

Plan

Furness Railway
Coniston Engine Shed

0   5   10   15   20   25   30 Feet

North elevation

East elevation

Drawn by Mike Faulkner, based on plans at Barrow Record Office

Later Plans

The Coniston branch was destined to change very little during its life of just over a hundred years. However there were plans for extensions and connections developed in the Light Railway era. In 1896 the Westmorland County Council Light Railway Committee placed before the Furness Railway Board a plan for a Coniston & Elterwater Light Railway to run via Tilberthwaite to tap quarries and a gunpowder works. The Furness Railway Directors at their meeting of 26th November 1896 agreed to work the line if built. It was never constructed.

Similarly, in 1901 a Greenodd & Lakebank Light Railway scheme was promoted by G Noble Fell, son of J B Fell, to run from a junction with the Lakeside branch at Greenodd to the Furness Railway pier at Coniston Lake Bank. The Furness Railway Directors at their meeting on 25th April 1901 again offered moral support but no capital, and funds sufficient for the project were never raised.

A small boost to traffic and revenue was the introduction during 1934 of camping coaches at Coniston and Torver. Initially three coaches were provided at Coniston, and they were stabled on the siding alongside the line to the Copperhouse north of the station. Another such vehicle was stationed at Torver. After the war, there were coaches only at Coniston, and these too disappeared at the end of the 1957 season. As part of the conditions of use, campers had to purchase four adult return tickets from their local station to their holiday destination. They would find a carriage 50 to 60 feet long, complete with sleeping and dining accommodation The charge in 1939 varied from £2 to £4 depending on the week the holiday was taken..

After closure to freight traffic in 1962 the remaining freight traffic was handled at Foxfield. Here it was proposed to build a new freight depot on the site of the former branch and sidings track bed. This proposal came to nothing and light industrial units now occupy the site.

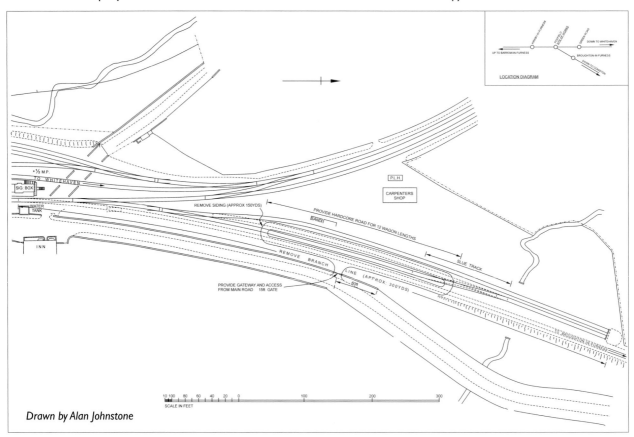

Drawn by Alan Johnstone

Proposed Goods Yard at Foxfield, 1960. *From a plan, prepared by the Divisional Engineers Office at Barrow No. BW/186/60 and dated 25th November 1960, shows the facilities promised at the time of closure. It would have utilised sidings alongside the branch and the connection to the main line. Sadly it was never built, but the gateposts are still present in the wall alongside the main road through Foxfield.*

The Board of Trade report on the inspection of the Coniston Railway stated that the line would be worked on the 'one engine in steam' principle. The line was to be divided into three sections for this purpose: Broughton - Woodland, Woodland - Torver and Torver - Coniston. Each section would have its own token or staff, which would be given to the train driver as his authority to enter the single line section.

The Inspecting Officer's report also noted that signals had been provided at each of the stations. These followed the practice of the day, consisting of a station signal at the station and 'distant' signals on the approach to it. The station signals consisted of a single post with two semaphore arms, one for each direction. The arms were worked by hand levers at the bottom of the post, and were capable of showing three positions. A horizontal arm indicated 'danger', an arm at 45 degrees downward 'caution' and an arm at 90 degrees within a slot in the post 'clear'. At night these three positions were shown by red, green and white lights. The danger signal indicated to the driver of an approaching train that the station was occupied, the caution signal that a train had just left, and the clear that the approved time interval had passed since the last train had left the station. The FR Capital Accounts indicate that the signals were supplied by Stevens & Company of London, then a leading manufacturer of railway signals.

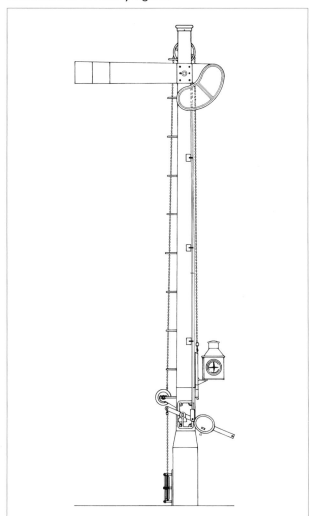

At the time of opening of the line to Coniston no telegraph was provided. The line in consequence had to be worked strictly according to the timetable. Out-of-course train movements had to be advised to the stationmasters by written notice conveyed by a previous train.

The first stationmaster at Coniston maintained a book into which he pasted the various notices received from headquarters in Barrow. In October 1863 he received a copy of the 1857 'Furness & Ulverstone & Lancaster Railways Electric Telegraph Instructions'. This suggests that the 'speaking telegraph' had been introduced on the Coniston Branch at that time. The instruments were of the 'double needle' type first introduced by Cooke & Wheatstone some 20 years previously. As well as being employed for messages they were used to advise the departure of trains to the next station. On 20th February 1871 the double needle telegraphs were replaced on the Furness Railway by the more versatile 'single needle' telegraphs on which two metal sounders allowed use of the Morse Code. Separate telegraph instruments exclusively for signalling trains were introduced throughout the Furness Railway on 10th January 1872.

An insight into the standards of operating practice in the early years of the Coniston Branch can be had from the account of an accident at Foxfield on 14th December 1861 published in the Ulverston Advertiser of 19th December:

> The Whitehaven engine had left its train of carriages in the proper place and had shunted out of the way onto the Coniston Branch. The Furness engine arrived and left its train in the proper place. The Furness engine had then to take the Coniston train and it is usual to attach to the front of this engine a goods van for Broughton and it is the duty of the stoker to hook on this van and then unhook it at Broughton where it is pushed into the goods siding.
>
> The Coniston train being ready to start with the stoker on the buffers ready to uncouple the van it started. Unfortunately the Whitehaven engine was only then shunting off the Coniston line and the two engines came into fearful collision, the van between them killing the stoker instantly. The driver of the Whitehaven engine, seeing that a collision was inevitable, reversed his engine and jumped off. The engine thus reversed started off up the Coniston line coming to a stand at Woodland for want of steam.

A number of serious accidents on the railways of Great Britain in the 1870s brought public demand for action and in 1889 legislation was brought in which made safety standards compulsory. The Regulation of Railways Act 1889 required interlocking of points and signals, block working on passenger lines and continuous brakes on passenger

Typical Furness Railway signal, c.1903. A wooden-post signal, typical of those erected by the Furness Railway around the turn of the century. This example was erected in 1903 as part of the re-signalling at Broughton, and was situated at the Coniston end of the down platform. (Mike Faulkner, based on photograph in Geoff Holme collection)

Coniston signal box, *c.1905. The attractive box which controlled the station at Coniston is seen here shortly after being brought to Coniston from Carnforth, a new box being built at Carnforth F&M Junction.* (Geoff Holme collection)

Furness Railway shunting signal of c.1896. *A rotating shunting signal, controlling movements from the outer platform at Coniston to the engine shed. The signal is in the 'Danger' position, showing a red aspect to the driver (a red lamp mounted on a red face). To show 'Clear', the signal would rotate to show a white aspect. These were very common in late Furness Railway signalling installations, and a few survived, as here, well into BR days.*
(CRA Alan Headech collection HEA 091)

Coniston North ground frame cabin, *c.1958. This cabin controlled the northern throat of the station, allowing engines to run round their trains. Notice the gong to the right of the door. The cabin building has now been preserved and still operates signals.(Hugh Oliver, Ken Norman collection ONA 11)*

Coniston North ground frame gong, *connected to lever No. 36 in the main signal box, and used to communicate with the operator of the ground frame.*
(Hugh Oliver, Ken Norman collection ONA 13)

vehicles. Each company was given a time limit to complete this work. Few companies complied with this requirement within the time-scale. The re-signalling of the Coniston Branch was not completed by the Furness Railway until 1897. Coniston station was enlarged and a new interlocking signalbox of 36 levers was opened on 24th May 1897. Torver ceased to be a block post and a ground frame was provided to control entry to the siding. At Woodland a loop with a second platform was operated by a new signalbox.

At Broughton there was no space for a loop and second platform opposite the existing platform and, although a new signalbox was provided, the practice of shunting one train into the sidings to allow the crossing of trains was continued. Col. Yorke of the Board of Trade Railway Department inspected the new signalling arrangements on the Coniston Branch on 16th July 1898. He required that the crossing of trains at Broughton must cease until a loop and second platform had been provided. In the spring of 1903 the FR realised that it would not be able to work the proposed summer service on the branch without crossing trains at Broughton. This was accomplished by building the loop and second platform staggered at the Foxfield end of the existing station.

The 1897 re-signalling of the Coniston Branch provided an opportunity to upgrade the block working by the introduction of Tyer's Electric Tablet system. The original 'one engine in steam' working had been superseded by 'Staff and Ticket'. This was more flexible as, when a second train was to follow on the single line, the driver of the first train was given a 'ticket' to proceed and was shown the staff. The staff was then carried by the driver of the second train. Unfortunately, the system was vulnerable to human failure. In 1870 the signal engineer and contractor, Edward Tyer, combined the staff and the block telegraph. The telegraph instruments at each end of a single line section contained a number of 'tablets' (so called because of their shape), only one of which could be taken out at either end at a time as the driver's authority to enter the single line section. The Furness Railway introduced Tyer's No. 6 tablet instruments on the Coniston Branch on 31st May 1897.

Woodland down distant signal, *c.1935. This signal, 24'-6" high, was 1161 yards from the signal box and erected in 1897 as part of the branch re-signalling. When photographed, it still retained its original lower quadrant arm and spectacle plate.*
(CRA Pattinson collection PA 0257)

Foxfield branch signal, *c.1935. These signals outside the Station House were provided to authorise movement from the up platform, either to Millom and the north or onto the branch. The shunting signals at the base allowed trains into the sidings alongside the branch. The building in the background is the former engine shed, trackless and long used for other purposes.*
(CRA Pattinson collection PA 0242)

Coniston Home signals, *c.1950. Situated at the southern end of the station, the imposing three-doll bracket signal admitted trains to platforms 1, 2 or 3. Trains to the goods yard were signalled by the upper arm on the single-post signal on the right of the photograph, while the lower arm signalled southbound departures from Coniston on the single-line section to Woodland.* *(Alan Pearsall)*

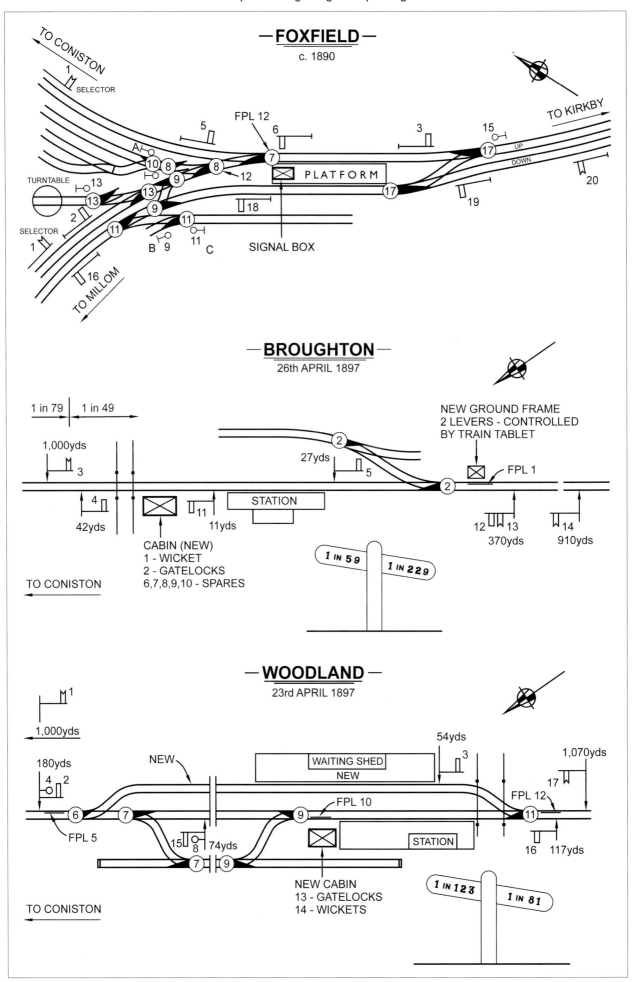

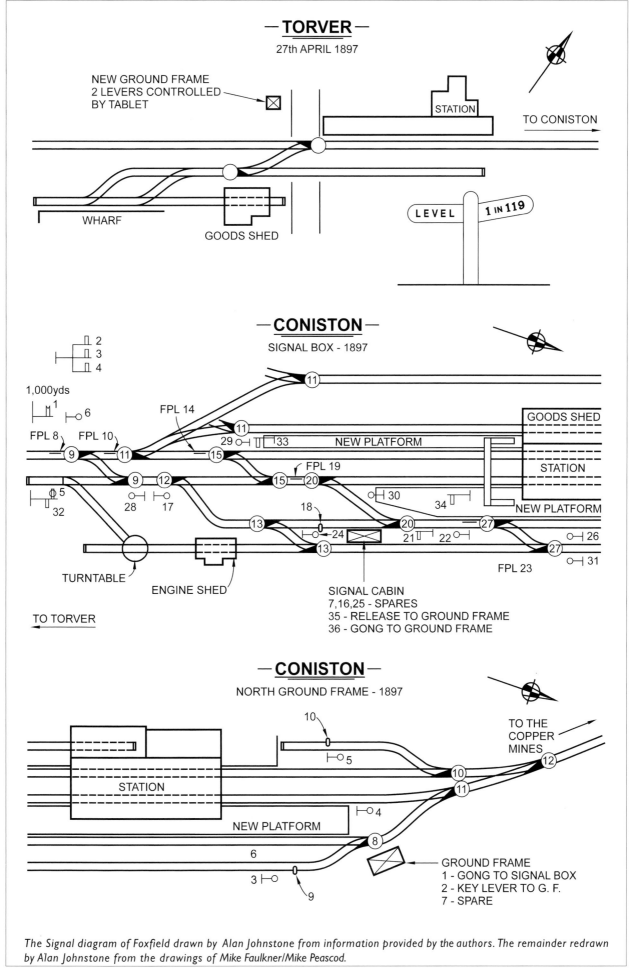

—TORVER—

27th APRIL 1897

NEW GROUND FRAME
2 LEVERS CONTROLLED
BY TABLET

STATION

TO CONISTON

WHARF

GOODS SHED

LEVEL   1 IN 119

—CONISTON—

SIGNAL BOX - 1897

1,000yds

FPL 14

FPL 8   FPL 10

FPL 19

GOODS SHED

NEW PLATFORM

STATION

NEW PLATFORM

TURNTABLE

ENGINE SHED

SIGNAL CABIN
7,16,25 - SPARES
35 - RELEASE TO GROUND FRAME
36 - GONG TO GROUND FRAME

FPL 23

TO TORVER

—CONISTON—

NORTH GROUND FRAME - 1897

TO THE
COPPER
MINES

STATION

NEW PLATFORM

GROUND FRAME
1 - GONG TO SIGNAL BOX
2 - KEY LEVER TO G. F.
7 - SPARE

The Signal diagram of Foxfield drawn by Alan Johnstone from information provided by the authors. The remainder redrawn by Alan Johnstone from the drawings of Mike Faulkner/Mike Peascod.

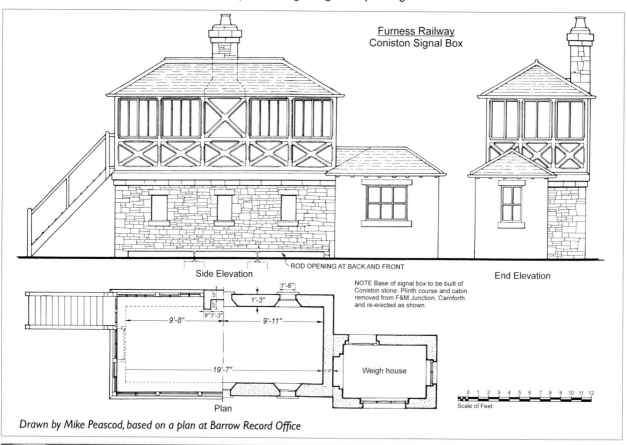

Furness Railway
Coniston Signal Box

Side Elevation

ROD OPENING AT BACK AND FRONT

End Elevation

NOTE Base of signal box to be built of Coniston stone. Plinth course and cabin removed from F&M Junction, Carnforth and re-erected as shown.

1'-6"
1'-3"
9'-8"
9'-11"
9"
1'-3"
19'-7"

Weigh house

0 1 2 3 4 5 6 7 8 9 10 11 12
Scale of Feet

Plan

Drawn by Mike Peascod, based on a plan at Barrow Record Office

Coniston signal box interior. *The box is seen here in the clean and polished condition in which signal boxes were always kept in those far-off days. The lever pull plates, indicating to the signalman which signal or points the lever operated, were made from cast brass and always shone. The layout of the area controlled by the box is indicated by the diagram mounted on the wall above the levers and the instrument containing the tablets for the single-line section to Woodland can be seen on the left.* (John Hext collection)

Passenger Services

The Kirkby to Broughton section opened in February 1848, and the timetable published for April 1848 shows just two trains on the Broughton extension, both running in connection with the boat between Fleetwood and Piel Pier. The boat left Fleetwood at 11 am and the train departed from Piel at 1 pm for Furness Abbey. Furness Abbey was at this period the focal point of the Furness Railway, the Piel, Barrow, Dalton and Broughton lines all meeting there. A train ran from Furness Abbey calling at Kirkby at 1.35 pm and arriving at Broughton at 1.45 pm. The southbound service left Broughton at 1.50 pm and a connecting service ran to Piel for the boat which reached Fleetwood at 5 pm.

In the summer of 1848 the steamer made two round trips between Fleetwood and Piel Pier. There were then four trains on the Broughton line. The two in the northbound direction, 11.50 am and 3.40 pm from Furness Abbey, were both steamer connections. Southbound, only the 1.30 pm from Broughton served the boat, as the 4 pm from Broughton ran to Barrow. The Furness Railway at this date had only four locomotives, so it is not surprising that several of the trains were mixed passenger and freight.

On 30th October 1850 the last section of the Whitehaven & Furness Junction Railway was ceremonially opened through to Broughton and from 1st November 1850 there were three trains each way on weekdays. In the up direction departures from Whitehaven were at 7.15 am, 10.30 am and 5.00 pm, the 10.30 am being in connection with the Fleetwood boat. Fifteen minutes were allowed for changing trains at Broughton. Similar services ran in the down direction.

From 1st August 1858 Foxfield Junction station appeared in the timetable and when the Coniston Railway opened on 18th June 1859 the Furness Railway main line was shown as between Coniston Lake and Barrow.

The train service for down trains in 1865 is shown in this timetable extract, taken from the 'Soulby's Ulverston Advertiser' of 6th May:

THE FURNESS RAILWAYS.

TIME TABLE FOR MAY, 1865.

	DOWN.	1 1 2 3 class	2 1 2 3 class	3 1 2 3 class	4 1 2 3 class	5 1 & 2 Exp.	6 1 2 3 class	1 1 2 3 class	2 1,2,3 class	3 1 2 3 class	4 1 2 3 class	5 1 2 3 class	FARES. From Lancaster. Ord. 1st		2nd		3rd.	
		p. m.	a. m.	a. m.	a. m.	a. m.	a. m.	a. m.	a. m.	p. m.	p.m.	a. m.	s.	d.	s.	d.	s.	d.
London & Nor. Western line	London........ *Depart*	....	....	....	....	9 0	1120	....	....	....	....	10 0						
	Birmingham..........	....	....	....	6 0	1115	1 45	....	....	....	....	1 5						
	Liverpool...*Lime-Street*	....	....	6 0	9 10	1 0	4 10	....	....	....	....	....						
	Liverpool (*Exchange St.*)	....	....	7 5	9 25	1 25	5 0	....	....	....	....	1 0						
	Manchester..... *L. & Y.*	....	....	6 20	9 30	1 40	4†40	....	....	....	....	1 0						
	,, *L. & N. W.*	....	....	....	9 30	1 0	4 30	....	....	....	....	....						
	Preston..............	....	....	8 0	1050	2 45	6 0	....	7 30	....	....	5 55						
	Leeds	....	....	5 35	....	1120	4 0	....	....	....	....	....						
	Kendal..............	....	....	....	9 45	....	6 20	....	....	....	....	6 5						
	Lancaster..........	....	....	9 0	1132	3 40	6 42	....	8 28	....	....	6 53						
	Carnforth *arrive* South	....	....	9 21	1146	3 55	6 57	....	8 48	....	....	7 13						
	,, ,, *North*	....	....	....	1048	....	7 4	....	....	....	....	6 52						
		a. m.	a. m.	a. m.	a. m.	p. m.	p. m.	a. m.	a. m.	p. m.	p.m.	p. m.						
	Carnforth........ *Depart*	....	....	9 35	1155	4 0	7 10	....	9 0	....	....	7 20	1	6	1	0	0	6½
	Silverdale..............	..	....	9 45	12 5	A	7 20	....	9 10	....	....	7 30	2	4	1	7	0	10½
	Arnside................	..	....	9 52	1212	....	A	....	9 18	....	....	7 37						
	Grange	....	....	10 0	1220	4 25	7 35	....	9 26	....	....	7 45	3	9	2	6	1	4½
	Kents Bank.........	....	....	10 7	1227	....	A	....	9 34	....	..	7 50						
	Cark and Cartmel.	....	....	1015	1235	4 35	7 45	...	9 42	....	....	8 0	4	6	3	2	1	8½
	Ulverstone	6 40	9 10	1030	1250	4 50	8 5	8 0	10 0	6 0	7 50	8 20	5	6	3	10	2	1½
	Lindal..................	6 50	9 20	1040	1 0	A	8 15	8 10	1010	6 10	8 0	8 30	6	2	4	4	2	4½
	Dalton..................	6 55	9 30	1045	1 5	5 5	8 20	8 15	1015	6 15	8 5	8 35	6	6	4	6	2	6
Barrow Branch	Furness Abbey......	7 0	9 35	1050	1 10	5 10	8 25	8 20	1020	6 20	8 10	8 40						
	Roose...............	....	A	A	A	A	A	....	A	....	A	A						
	Barrow.......*Arrive*	...	9 45	11 0	1 20	5 25	8 35	....	1030	....	8 20	8 50						
	Barrow ....*Depart*	6 50	....	1040	....	5 0	....	7 20	....	5 15	....	....	7	4	5	4	2	10
	Roose...............	....	....	A	....	A	....	A	....	....	....	....						
	Furness Abbey.......	7 5	....	1055	....	5 15	....	8 25	....	6 25	....	....	6	9	4	10	2	7½
	Kirkby	7 20	....	1110	....	5 30	....	8 45	....	6 40	....	....	7	10	5	10	3	1
	Foxfield Junction	7 30	....	1120	....	5 35	....	8 55	....	6 50	....	....	8	5	6	2	3	3½
	Broughton	7 35	....	1130	....	5 45	....	9 0	....	6 55	....	....	8	8	6	4	3	4½
	Woodland................	7 42	....	1140	....	A	....	9 10	....	7 5	....	....						
	Torver..................	7 50	....	1152	....	6 0	....	9 20	....	7 15	....	....						
	Coniston Lake (arrive)..	8 0	....	12 0	....	6 10	....	9 30	....	7 25	....	....	10	8	7	10	4	1½
Whitehaven Line.	Foxfield .... *Depart*	7 30	....	1120	....	5 40	....	9 0	....	6 55	....	....						
	Drigg ..*Wastwater*	8 26	....	1217	....	6 31	....	9 56	....	7 51	....	....						
	Whitehaven........	9 15	....	1 5	....	7 15	....	1045	....	8 40	....	....	16	0	12	2	6	3½
	Workington........	11 0	....	3 19	....	7 59	....	2 24	....	....	....	....						
	Cockermouth	1130	....	5 30	....	8 30	....	8 20	....	....	....	....	19	0	14	2	7	7

A Stops by Signal if required. — B stops to take up passengers going north or south of Carnforth.
† This Train will leave Manchester at 4 p.m. on Saturdays.

By the time the Furness & Midland line was opened and steamer services between Piel Pier, Belfast and Douglas had been inaugurated in 1867, the Furness Railway timetable indicated a main line between Carnforth and Whitehaven, with the Barrow and Coniston lines as branches. On the Coniston branch in September 1867, there were six trains in each direction on weekdays. The day started with the 6.40 am from Coniston Lake, while the last train of the day ran from Foxfield Junction, terminating at Broughton at 7.40 pm. Two additional trips between Foxfield Junction and Broughton were undertaken during the day, the timetable being designed to allow a convenient connection at Foxfield Junction either north or south for each train. On Sundays, three trains each way made similar connections.

After the opening on 1st June 1882 of the Barrow Loop line and Barrow Central station, Foxfield to Coniston (now plain Coniston) was again shown as a branch (from plain Foxfield).

In the summer of 1907, at the height of the Aslett era (Alfred Aslett was appointed Furness Railway General Manager in 1895 and actively promoted the tourist traffic), there were eight trains each way between Foxfield and Coniston and three between Foxfield and Broughton. Notable were the 'Fleetwood Boat Trains' running in connection with the Furness Railway steamer service between Fleetwood and Ramsden Dock, Barrow. The down train left Ramsden dock station at 12.05 pm, and the up train departed Coniston at 6 pm. These trains were used by passengers booked on the Outer Circular Tour (Lakeside, Ambleside and Coniston) and the Inner Circular Tour (Furness Abbey, Greenodd and Coniston).

For the long suffering patrons of the Thursday Ulverston Market, that social high point of the Furness week then as now, a Thursday only train left Coniston at 8.35 am for Broughton and Foxfield. There it connected with the 9.00 am from Millom to Carnforth giving an arrival at Ulverston at 10.11 am.

The summer public timetable for June, July and August, 1907 (John Hext collection) is shown:

CONISTON BRANCH
WITH CONNECTIONS.

DOWN.	WEEK DAYS.											SUNDAYS.		
	1	2	3	4	5	6	7	8	9	10	11	1	2	3
	a.m.	a.m.	a.m.	a.m.	p.m.	p.m.	p.m.	p.m.	p.m.	p.m.	p.m.	a.m.	p.m.	p.m.
Carnforth ......dep.	4 25	7 0	...	9 50	...	1 5	1 28	...	4 53	...	6 10	7 35	...	...
Grange ....,,	...	7 25	...	9 55	...	12 35	1 53	...	4 30	...	6 35	8 0	THRO' TRAIN TO CONISTON.	—
Ulverston ......,,	4 57	7 52	...	10 22	...	1 33	2 20	...	5 23	...	7 2	8 27		6 17
Dalton ....,,	5 8	8 5	...	10 35	...	1 9	2 33	...	5 15	...	7 15	8 40		6 30
Furness Abbey ,,	...	8 10	...	10 40	—	1 47	2 38	...	5 20	...	7 20	8 45		6 35
Barrow (Dock) ,,	...	7 A 10	...	...	12 5	...	...	...	...	...	6 D 10	...		6 10
Barrow (Central ,,	5 23	8 25	—	11 0	12 30	2 0	2 53	—	5 55	—	7 35	9 0	2 30	6 50
Whitehaven (Bransty)	6 40	6 40	8 E 5	10 25	11 40	...	2 45	3F 30	3F 30	5 40	5 40	8 30	...	5 40
Millom........,,	8 0	8 0	9 0	11 40	12 41	...	3 38	4 55	4 55	6 55	6 55	9 45	...	6 55
FOXFIELD depart	8 15	8 55	9 15	11 55	12 55	2 35	3 50	5 20	6 35	7 10	8 5	10 0	3 0	7 20
Broughton... ,,	8 18	8 58	9 19	12 0	12 58	2 38	3 55	5 23	6 38	7 14	8 10	10 3	3 7	7 23
Woodland ... ,,	—	9 5	...	12 8	...	...	4 3	—	6 45	—	8 18	10 10	3 10	7 30
Torver ...... ,,	...	9 13	...	12 18	...	...	4 13	...	6 53	...	8 28	10 18	3 18	7 38
CONISTON...arrive	...	9 20	9 40	12 25	1 15	2 55	4 20	...	7 0	...	8 35	10 25	3 25	7 45

UP.	WEEK DAYS.											SUN.		
	1	2	3	4	5	6	7	8	9	10	11	1	2	3
	a.m.	a.m.	a.m.	a.m.	a.m.	p.m.	p.m	p.m	p.m.	p.m.	p.m.	a.m.	p.m.	p.m.
CONISTON......dep.	7 40	...	8 35	10 50	11 55	2 25	4 25	6 0	6 25	...	7 50	9 0	6 35	7 50
Torver .... ,,	7 46	...	8 42	10 57	12 1	2 32	4 31	...	6 32	...	7 56	9 6	6 41	7 56
Woodland........ ,,	7 54	—	8 53	11 8	12 9	2 43	4 39	...	6 43	—	8 4	9 14	6 49	8 4
Broughton ..... ,,	8 2	8 42	9 1	11 16	12 17	2 51	4 47	6 17	6 51	7 51	8 12	9 22	6 57	8 12
FOXFIELD......arr.	8 5	8 45	9 5	11 20	12 20	2 55	4 50	6 20	6 55	7 55	8 15	9 25	7 0	8 15
Millom ....arr.	9 3	9 3	...	11 38	2 G 31	3 34	5 3	6 36	8 13	8 13	8 41	9 41	7 31	......
Whitehaven ... ,, (Bransty)	10 7	10 7	...	12 50	3 25	4 50	6 15	...	9 55	9 55	9 55	10 55	8 45	......
Barrow (Central ,,	8 40	9 40	9 40	12 20	1 10	3 35	5 35	6 42	7 35	—	8 45	10 25	7 35	8 45
Barrow (Dock ... ,,	8 55	...	...	...	1 H 50	...	...	6 55	8 A 20	...	...	...		
Furness Abbey.. ,,	8 55	9 53	9 53	12 35	2 0	3 50	5 50	7 3	7 50	...	...	10 40	7 50	
Dalton ....,,	9 0	9 58	9 58	12 40	2 5	3 55	5 55	7 8	7 55	...	9 10	10 45	7 55	
Ulverston ......,,	9 13	10 11	10 11	12 53	1 35	4 8	6 8	7 18	8 8	...	9 20	10 58	9 8	
Grange ....,,	9 37	10 33	10 33	1 17	2 42	4 32	6 32	7 35	8 32	...	9 C 55	5 37	8 32	
Carnforth.......,,	10 5	10 55	10 55	1 45	2 7	5 07	0 7	7 52	9 0	...	9 52	6 59	0 7	THRO' TRAIN FROM CONISTON.

A—Tuesdays, Thursdays and Saturdays only.   B—Leaves Whitehaven 3-30 p.m. on Thursdays.   C—Stops when required only.   D—Daily till August 31st and Thursdays and Saturdays only commencing September 5th.   E—Corkickle Station.   F—Thursdays only.   G—2-18 p.m. on Saturdays.   H—Daily till September 7th and Thursdays and Saturdays only commencing September 12th.

During the last years of World War I, workmen's trains ran between Coniston and Barrow Shipyard.

The typical LMS passenger service on the Coniston branch varied little. For August 1930, Bradshaw shows 10 trains each way on weekdays. From 15th January 1934, one class motor trains (push-pull) were introduced. In the summer timetable of 1939, a train left Blackpool Central at 8.50 am, arriving at Coniston at 12.11 pm. It returned from Coniston at 6 pm. These trains used the Dalton Loop line, so avoiding Barrow. On Saturdays the train started at Carnforth and returned to Morecambe Promenade.

The final era of the Coniston branch was largely a motor train operation. There were about nine trains each way on weekdays but in the summer timetable there was a through train from Blackpool to Coniston on Tuesdays and Thursdays only, arriving at around midday and returning to Blackpool in the evening. This train, rostered for a Class 5, the largest locomotives normally to use the branch, had the distinction of being the only regular passenger train in BR days to run via the Dalton Loop line between Dalton Junction and Park South. On one occasion at least, a 'Jubilee' appeared. On 18th July 1957, No. 45678 *De Robeck* had a leaking cylinder gland. It was replaced on its rostered Glasgow working by the Class 5 originally intended for Coniston, the 'Jubilee' going to Coniston in its stead. Driver Slater and Fireman Beck, of Carnforth shed, nursed the engine carefully and ensured a safe return for the passengers on this trip.

The Sunday service for many years consisted of two trains a day each way. These were worked by the branch engine, and connected at Foxfield with the two trains which formed the Sunday service on the northern section of the main line. In the later days of the Furness Railway, this service was augmented in summer by a through train from Barrow, which left in the early afternoon and returned in the late evening. From the start of World War I, this train was discontinued. Indeed, no service at all was provided on Sundays during 1917 and 1918, except that the April 1918 timetable showed the curious arrangement of an empty train being sent from Barrow to form an evening train from Coniston back to Barrow.

By the summer of 1922, four Sunday trains were provided. In the morning, the branch engine worked two trips to Foxfield and back, the second of these being for the benefit of passengers from the north. In the afternoon, a Barrow engine operated to Coniston, returning to Barrow in the evening, and having made a trip to Foxfield in the meantime. Such a service continued in LMS days, with the object of catering for those who wished to seek the fells and lakes. The winter service, however, was discontinued even before the depression years of the 1930s.

The summer service continued through the years of World War II, though, in common with many other holiday services, it was cancelled in 1944 as D-Day approached. After the war, there were usually only three trains each way, two of these being through services from Barrow. The Sunday service did not always run for the full period of the summer timetable, but it always started from the Whitsuntide holiday.

While the Lakeside branch was frequently host to specials, these seem to have been rare on the Coniston line. The Special Train Notice for the August Bank Holiday week of 1939 contains none to Coniston, and that for the Whit Bank Holiday of 1955 only one, a modest Barrow to Coniston and return.

Coniston station, c. 1905. *Against a magnificent background the stationmaster is watching the railmotor and trailer at Coniston in the line's golden heyday. The sharply curved outer excursion platform, so unpopular with the operators, can be clearly seen. (Wyn Anderson collection)*

Freight Services

Little is known about the early freight traffic on the Coniston branch other than that in those days most trains were 'mixed', passenger and freight. Neither is it clear how much of the copper ore traffic, the original reason for building the line, was carried. The tonnages for Coniston copper ore and slate production for 1865 were 250 and 2,000 respectively. These were small amounts compared with the amount of iron ore carried at this time. Nevertheless, when the future of the 1865 Duddon crossing scheme was being critically examined by the Furness Railway Board on 27th October 1868, it was recorded that, of the 30,000 train miles per annum on the 6½ extra miles of the existing route via Foxfield, no less than 18,000 were Coniston traffic.

The earliest available Working Timetable, that of January 1877, indicates that the Coniston branch was served by one train a day, the 8.20 am roadside goods from Carnforth to Coniston and return. By June 1908 the Coniston goods had become a Barrow working, which departed from Barrow Yard at 12.05 pm and arrived at Coniston at 3.20 pm. It left at 4.45 pm, arriving at Barrow at 7.05 pm. In the early LMS days a similar train ran, departing from Barrow Yard at 9.00 am and returning from Coniston at 2 pm. This train continued virtually unchanged, except for being reduced to Mondays, Wednesdays and Fridays only, until the line was closed for passenger traffic on 6th October 1958. Thereafter it became a three days a week extension of 'Target 18', which had long served sidings on the St. Luke's Loop, Dawson's timber yard off the Hawcoat branch, Park and Askam Brick Works. The Coniston branch finally closed to all traffic on 30th April 1962 and lifting of the permanent way began soon afterwards.

Branch freight train, *c.1910. Sharp, Stewart 0-6-0 No. 118 is seen passing Coniston signal box with a freight train. The locomotive was built in 1881, was rebuilt with a larger boiler in 1906, and continued to work until 1927. The first wagon is covered by a Furness Railway wagon sheet, provided by the company for its customers.* (Wyn Anderson collection)

When the Coniston Railway opened, the Furness Railway had just two basic types of locomotive. There were the 0-4-0 locomotives of the 'Bury' design, typified by No. 3, *Coppernob*, in the National Railway Museum. For passenger services, there were the little 2-2-2 'Well Tanks' built by Sharp Brothers, Manchester, but there were only four of these. Perhaps the 'Bury' locomotives were pressed into service for passenger or mixed turns on the Coniston line, but, with the delivery of further tank engines in the 1860s, it seems likely that these became the mainstay of passenger traffic in the early years. No. 37 is featured in the photograph taken on the branch in the 1870s, reproduced on page 48, and showing the locomotive at the head of a train of 4-wheeled carriages. The leading vehicles are smartly turned out in the livery of the period: cream and crimson lake for panelled carriages, the 3rd class vehicles out of sight being in varnished deal and oak or teak.

Main line passenger trains in the 1870s and 80s were in the hands of a class of 2-4-0 locomotives built by Sharp, Stewart & Co of Manchester (successors of Sharp Brothers, builders of the 2-2-2WTs). When loads became heavier and they were beginning to be replaced by the larger 4-4-0 locomotives, some of them were rebuilt into tank locomotives, a pony truck under the bunker converting them into a 2-4-2, and making them ideal for branch line use. Nos. 73 and 74 of this class certainly appeared at Coniston. A photograph taken inside the train shed at Coniston, and seen on page 32, shows No. 73 with another train of early 4-wheeled carriages, this time in the later livery of chocolate brown for the panelled stock. The 4-wheeled carriages would remain in service for a few more years yet, before being displaced by 6-wheeled carriages in the remaining years of the century in yet another livery of ultramarine and white.

In the early years of the 20th century, companies were seeking economies, and operating a branch passenger service by 'steam rail motor car' was seen as a way forward. Basically, this was a passenger coach and engine combined; it could be driven from either end, and could cope with a small amount of 'tail traffic' if extra passengers needed to be carried. Mr Pettigrew, the company's Locomotive Superintendent, had already prepared drawings of a suitable vehicle. The Great Western Railway was experimenting with such a rail motor between Chalford and Stonehouse in the Stroud Valley. As soon as it was clear that significant economies could be achieved, construction was sanctioned to Mr Pettigrew's design at an estimated cost of £2,000. Built in the company's own workshops, it was intended for use on either the Lakeside or the Coniston branches. A trailer car was also constructed.

Publicity material of the day extolled the *handsome design*, mentioning that the twelve first-class passengers would have the benefit of moquette seats, the thirty-six third-class passengers having to make do with rattan. The Trailer

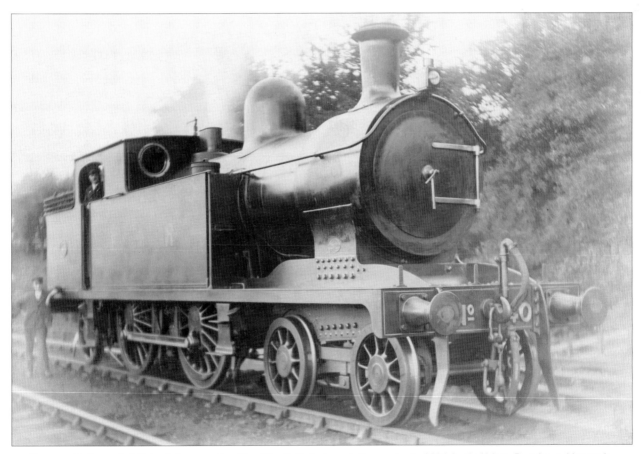

Furness Railway 4-4-2 tank locomotive No. 40. Built for branch line service in 1916 by the Vulcan Foundry at Newton-le-Willows, No. 40 was one of a small class of six locomotives. Here she is seen at Coniston with the branch line guard Willy Reddon standing on the footplate.

(John Hext collection)

accommodated a further thirty-four third-class passengers, and there was sufficient power available to haul a horse box in addition. On completion, it was put to work on the Lakeside branch at Easter, 1905. Initially, there were problems of oscillation and vibration of the car. Improvements were made, and the rail motor then made its appearance on the Coniston line, operating throughout the months of July, August and September.

Complaints from the influential Lakeside patrons led to the rail motor's continued use on the Coniston branch, though a smoking compartment was provided on the trailer for the use of first-class passengers. Only Mr W Barratt, Director of the Hodbarrow Mining Company and living in Broughton, ventured to complain, and this he did in the strongest possible terms. This extract gives a flavour:

> There can be no doubt whatever the thing is an absolute failure, at any rate on the Coniston section of your line with its steep gradients and also as regards the convenience and comfort of the travelling public.

The rail motor continued in use until the commencement of the Great War.

The 2-4-2 tanks were by now showing their age and were being helped out on occasions by 0-6-2 tanks as a stopgap. A completely new design was introduced in 1915, a new type of passenger tank engine designed by Pettigrew,

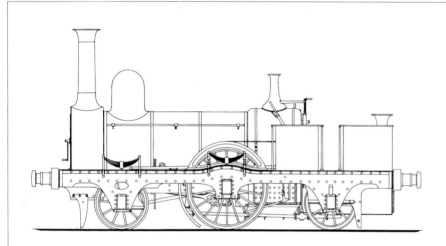

Some of the earlier train services on the branch were operated by single wheeled well-tank engines, and the drawing represents two built for the Furness Railway by Sharp Brothers, of Manchester. They were allocated the F.R. running numbers 11 & 12. No. 11 eventually went to the Watlington & Princes Risborough Railway and No. 12 found its way to the Weston, Clevedon & Portishead Railway. Photographs of this locomotive can be seen on pages 16 and 48.

The next stage in locomotive development brought some four-wheeled passenger engines onto the line, and when in turn these engines were later replaced by bogie passenger engines, some of them were converted into tank engines. They were admirably suited to branch line operation. A photograph of this locomotive can be seen on page 32.

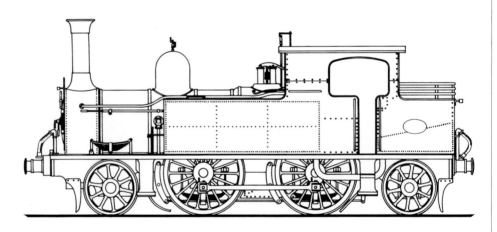

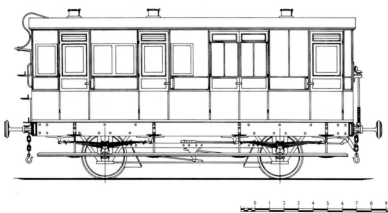

The early carriage stock of railways was always quite rudimentary, and this two-compartment brake composite carriage of 1864 is no exception. It was built by J Wright & Sons of Birmingham.

Drawings by Mike Peascod

Scale of feet
0 1 2 3 4 5 6 7 8 9 10

of the 4-4-2 wheel arrangement. Designed for use on the Kendal, Lakeside and Coniston branches, they were graceful machines with a useful turn of speed, and apparently coped well with the difficult gradients on the Coniston line. Nos. 40 and 42 are known to have worked the branch. Six of these engines were built, and they looked after the line's passenger needs well into LMS days.

Economies to reduce operating expenditure continued to be sought by the new company, and the earlier ideas embodied in the rail motor were applied to the 'Motor Train'. By means of linkages with the cab of the locomotive, brake and regulator could be controlled by the driver travelling in a cab in the end vehicle. As noted, motor train working, 3rd class only, was introduced from 15th January 1934, powered by Aspinall ex-L&Y 2-4-2 tank engines which had been transferred to Barrow and 'motor fitted'.

From about 1935, Fowler 2-6-2 tank engines were seen at Coniston, often having taken over the Blackpool-Coniston train at Ulverston. No. 67 was involved in a buffer-stop collision while running round at Coniston on 25th August 1939.

During World War II, the L&Y tanks were replaced on the motor trains by their ex-LNWR contemporaries, the smaller Webb 2-4-2 tank engines. The footplate canopy was so low that it is said a tall driver had difficulty keeping his hat on. Nos. 6682 and 6718 were the engines rostered for these duties. These engines were under-powered, and could only just manage a loaded two-coach train up the bank out of Broughton. These locomotives continued in use on the line until 1946, when L&Y tanks made a reappearance in the form of nos. 10643 and 10644.

The final motive power on the branch was provided by two Ivatt 2-6-2 tanks, No. 41221 in 1949 and 41217 in 1951. The Blackpool-Coniston service was worked throughout by Stanier Class 5 4-6-0s, and these had to run light to Millom to turn on the larger turntable there.

During August 1954 for a few weeks the steam-hauled Motor Train was replaced by an experimental 3-car diesel set of four-wheel units running in its manufacturers' colours of grey with red lining. They apparently did not acquit themselves too well, lack of adhesion on the banks and rough riding seeming to afflict them. However, the superior views and absence of smoke were much appreciated. Apart from this short experiment, which was not developed, all train services on the branch were steam hauled, and diesels only made a regular appearance on the branch when the Co-Bo diesels shedded at Barrow were in charge of the demolition trains.

Although the line was opened on the pretext of potentially large loads of copper ore, the output from the local mines soon diminished, to be overtaken by slate being loaded at Coniston and Torver. Thus, freight rolling stock would have been dominated by open wagons for copper ore (briefly), slate, coal, and general merchandise, with specially built covered wagons for explosives, covered wagons for flour and other cereals, bolster trucks for timber, and livestock wagons.

Railmotor at Coniston, c.1907. Here the railmotor can be seen at platform 2, framed by the arch at the northern end of the station. The trailer car can be seen leading the train. After withdrawal, the boiler was utilised to power the breakdown crane. The coach and trailer bodies were incorporated into dwellings at Rampside and Kirkby. *(Wyn Anderson collection)*

Sharp, Stewart 2-2-2 Well Tank No. 37, *c.1870, on a train of four-wheeled coaches at Coniston. This earliest known photograph of the branch shows the south end of the building before its extension further southwards. As built there was no glazed screen. The large building on the left is the goods shed, at that time a separate structure.* (George Taylor collection)

Fowler 2-6-2 Tank No. 1 *waits at Coniston to take the 6 pm return corridor express to Blackpool, c.1937. No. 1 will take the train via the Dalton Loop as far as Ulverston. No. 1 was employed for many years on less onerous duties as Barrow Central pilot.*
(Lance Kelly collection)

Coniston Lake had been used for hundreds of years before the arrival of the railway as a means of transport in this area. Copper ore from the mines on the slopes of Coniston Old Man, slate from the quarries in the Coniston area and on Walna Scar, iron produced by the many bloomeries sited along the shores of the lake, all were transported along Coniston Water to Nibthwaite. From here it was transhipped by road before being reloaded for forward transport by sea at Greenodd, which was an important port and shipbuilding centre before the coming of the railway. A small amount of gunpowder travelled in the opposite direction from Nibthwaite to Coniston. These activities only finally ceased when the Lakeside branch was built across the estuary in the late 1860s, irrevocably changing the tidal channels and siphoning away the remaining trade.

The first steam-propelled vessel to operate on the lake, according to a notice in Soulby's Ulverston Advertiser of 12th July 1855, was a small screw-propelled steamer named *Queen of the Lake*, which had been launched at High Nibthwaite. The notice announced that, from 16th July, she would ply from the Waterhead Inn at Coniston to High Nibthwaite, offering a passenger service.

It is believed that this vessel was transported in her completed state overland from Greenodd by a team of horses, so she cannot have been a large boat. On 16th August, just one month after commencing service, she was being offered for sale, suggesting that trade had not come up to expectations and that the venture had proved unprofitable. This is not surprising, as there would have been little demand for passenger travel in this remote part of the Lake District. It was the coming of the railway which opened the way for the tourist and the holidaymaker,

Quick to see the potential for a steamer service on the lake aimed mainly at the tourist market, the Furness Railway set one up within a few months of the opening of the Coniston Railway. At this early date the Furness Railway had no powers to operate such a service, a situation which persisted until the passing of the Furness Railway (Steamboats) Act 1872, when the Company purchased the Windermere services which had been operating since the 1840s. Consequently the vessel, which at the time was described as *resembling those known as the Gondolas of Venice*, was registered in the name of James Ramsden. Built by Jones, Quiggin and Co. of Liverpool at a cost of £1,200, she was transported to Coniston by rail in sections. After assembly, she was launched from Pier Cottage slipway, close to Coniston Old Hall. The ceremony took place on 1 December 1859, performed by Miss Boileau of Coniston, while James Ramsden knocked away the wedges which held the vessel on the slipway.

Described by the Illustrated London News as *the most elegant little steam vessel yet designed*, she was named *Gondola*, a name well suited to this *perfect combination of the Venetian gondola and the English steam yacht*. With her graceful lines and unique appearance, she captured the imagination of the public in a most remarkable way. Of riveted construction, built from Low Moor iron plates, this 42-ton vessel was 84 feet long with a beam of 14 feet 2 inches. Originally the exhaust was through ducts set in the stern.

Gondola, *c.1880. Seen at Lake Bank pier, at the southern end of the lake,* Gondola *is in her original condition prior to having her cabin shortened in 1903 to provide a cockpit at the stern.*
(Ruskin Museum, Coniston)

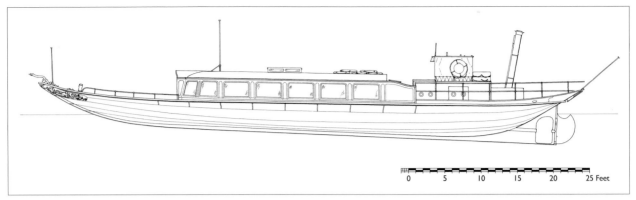

Gondola, *c.1981. The rebuilt vessel with the small alterations to the design required for modern sighting and safety standards.*
(Mike Faulkner)

When she was launched with a full head of steam, water rushed in and extinguished the fire, so it was thought prudent to fit a conventional raked funnel.

Internally she was finished in walnut with twin gilded Corinthian columns between the windows, which latter were draped with silk curtains. Interior decoration was in blue and white, the cabin being cushioned and carpeted after the style of a railway's royal coaches. Registered to carry 200 passengers, she had a gilded figurehead in the form of a serpent, bows with a sweeping curve bearing the motto of the Duke of Devonshire, *Cavendo Tutus*, a tripod-mounted mast and a clipper stern.

In 1900, the Smoking Room was removed and this, together with other alterations costing a total of £35, authorised by the Board Committee on 13th December 1900, made additional accommodation for second-class passengers. It is interesting to note that, as built, the cabin had eight windows on each side, but in 1903 the cabin length was reduced to provide a cockpit, and thereafter it only had seven windows.

The *Gondola* cruises round Coniston Lake ran in connection with the arrival of trains at Coniston station. In the 1860s, with the rapid expansion of Barrow's iron and steel industry and the resulting increase in freight traffic on the Furness line, the punctuality of the passenger trains deteriorated. A memorandum dated 19th June 1867 in the Coniston Rate Book reads:

> In future the Gondola must not sail from the pier before 12.30 pm in order to allow passengers time to get down from the train. A flag staff will be fixed at the station and when the train is more than half an hour late the flag will be hoisted for the Gondola to leave.

In 1870, much earlier than is usually appreciated and following the opening of the Lakeside branch in June 1869, Henry Cook, the Traffic Manager of the Furness Railway introduced 'Circular Tours in Lakeland'. There were initially three of these tours, and a real effort was made to integrate the various methods of transport, by road, rail and water. The Outer Circular Tour (No.1) was by train to Windermere Lake Side, by steamer to Ambleside, by coach from Ambleside to Coniston and then onward by train. The Inner Circular Tour (No. 2) took the tourist by train to Coniston, by *Gondola* to Lake Bank, by road to Greenodd and thence by train. The Middle Circular Tour (No. 4) went by train to Windermere Lake Side, by steamer to Ambleside, by coach to Coniston, by *Gondola* to Lake

Bank, by coach to Greenodd and then onward by train. All tours could be taken in the opposite direction and ran excluding Sundays. The tours were to be greatly extended at a later date by Alfred Aslett.

In 1871, *Gondola*, then only 12 years in service, was commanded by Captain Felix Hamill who remained her master until his retirement in 1921. For many years he lived in Pier Cottage adjacent to the slipway and it is estimated that during his lifetime on the vessel he made 13,000 sailings, causing damage amounting to only seven shillings and sixpence (37$\frac{1}{2}$ p) in that time. A model of *Gondola* built by Capt. Hamill can be seen today in the Ruskin Museum in Coniston village.

On 21st November 1906, the Furness Railway General Manager, Mr Alfred Aslett, submitted to his Board a memorandum on the Coniston Lake steamer traffic, which recorded the number of passengers carried on the *Gondola* as follows:

1897	14,264
1904	17,572
1905	19,125
1906	22,445

This rapid increase is quite remarkable and reflected the success of the tours and the general promotion of tourist traffic by Mr Aslett.

Based on the above returns, it was not surprising that Aslett declared another steamer for Coniston to be *absolutely necessary*. In 1907 the Board of the Furness Railway Company accepted a tender from John I Thornycroft of Southampton for a twin-screw steamer to be built in sections at their Woolston Yard on the south coast, this at a cost of £5,600. Transported to Coniston by rail for assembly, her launching took place on 20th May 1908, from the Pier Cottage slipway previously used for *Gondola*. Earlier, at its meeting on 22nd November 1907, the Furness Railway Board had decided to name this new vessel *Lady of the Lake*.

With a total length of 97 feet 6 inches, a beam of 15 feet and a depth of 6 feet 9 inches, her engines were mounted either side of a locomotive-type boiler of 120 lbs/sq.in. working pressure. Her top speed was 11$\frac{1}{2}$ knots. Two-decked with a spacious and well-ventilated cabin amidships, she was registered to carry 400 passengers. With her canoe-like prow and clipper stern, she bore a striking resemblance to the Windermere steam yacht *Tern*.

Lady of the Lake, c.1910. *Seen here moored at Waterhead pier, Coniston. Visible to the left of the vessel is Pier House cottage, the home for many years of Captain Hamill, the captain of* Gondola.   (Bruce Holme collection)

Lady of the Lake never attained the popularity of *Gondola*, which she was intended to replace but never did, neither with her passengers nor her crew. It is said that, with her engines placed in the stern, her bow rode high in the water, which made her difficult to steer in rough and windy weather.

Like *Gondola*, she appears to have had few mishaps, although on 27th May 1913, the Furness Railway's Traffic & Works Committee recorded an incident of her going aground at Lake Bank Pier, an event that had occurred on Wednesday, 14th May. On this occasion £28 worth of damage was caused when the newly appointed engineer, McDowell, misunderstood an order from the captain to alter the reversing levers to go astern. Consequently the vessel forged ahead and ran aground, causing £10 of damage to Lake Bank Pier.

In June 1908 there were six sailings each way between Waterhead and Lake Bank, but whilst the Windermere Lake steamers appeared in the Furness Main Line Timetable in Bradshaw, the Coniston steamers did not share this distinction.

For the 1909 season the Directors decided to run a lake service on Sundays during July, August and September, connecting with the Barrow to Coniston excursion trains. As a result of objections by Mr A P Brydson of Blawith, on whose land the Lake Bank Pier stood, the Furness Railway Board decided on 11th June not to stop at Lake Bank Pier on Sunday. This service was not a great success, as returns at the end of the season showed that, of the 4,215 passengers who used the excursion trains, just 637 sailed on the lake, and these gave a revenue of only £26. Despite these poor returns, the service was continued and an unsuccessful attempt made in 1911 to persuade Mr Brydson to allow Sunday sailings to call at Lake Bank Pier.

The proposed retirement of *Gondola* after 49 years' service did not occur and both vessels continued to sail until 1914. Then, on 12th August, at the outbreak of the Great War, *Lady of the Lake* was withdrawn from service, although it appears *Gondola* remained in service for the rest of the season. Initially it was intended to run her for a short season in 1915, but by 10th June the Furness Railway Board had decided to suspend any further sailings for the duration of the war. This decision was made despite taking into account the fact that only Capt. Hamill, an engineer and a boy were needed to crew the vessel. Mr Aslett had also pointed out that receipts would almost certainly be under the £57 per month working expenses incurred in the 1914 season. The assumption was based partly on the possible loss of revenue by having to discontinue Circular Tour No. 2 (the Inner Tour), which had operated since 1885, and Circular Tour No. 4 (the Middle Tour), which had operated since 1889. Both these tours required a lake steamer to connect with the road service from Lake Bank to Greenodd. This decision caused great inconvenience and a loss of trade to the boarding houses and village residents, but the Furness Railway Board meeting of 23rd July confirmed the decision of 10th June despite its having received a protest signed by 28 residents against the original decision.

Following a letter from Mr Joe Tyson of the Waterhead Hotel dated 5th May 1916, the Board considered, at its meeting of 12th May 1916, reinstating the service for the summer of that year. Once again it was decided not to run *Gondola*, a decision confirmed on 9th June despite two further protest letters.

After the war, sailing recommenced and both vessels returned to service. The London Midland and Scottish

Gondola, *c.1910. Moored at Waterhead pier. Pier House is to the right of the vessel. The stern of* Lady of the Lake *can be seen moored on the other side of the pier.* *(Alan Pearsall collection)*

Lady of the Lake, *c.1910. Steaming south down the lake towards Lake Bank.*

(G P Abraham 952, Peter Fleming collection)

Railway continued some of the Circular tours, with the road sections utilising Ribble Motors services. *Lady of the Lake* finally ceased operation on the outbreak of war in 1939. She was broken up for scrap in 1950.

Gondola was also taken out of service. Her engine was removed and sold in 1944, although it was believed it never saw further use. Subsequently a Barrow businessman purchased the hull, converted it into a houseboat, and moored it at the southern end of the lake near High Nibthwaite. *Gondola* thus remained in use as a houseboat until the winter of 1963-64, when she was sunk.

However, this was not the end of the story for this grand old vessel, which was by now over 100 years old. Mr Arthur Hatton purchased her for £40, her book value in 1908, and after removing her interior fittings, patched her hull sufficiently for her to be re-floated. He then beached her at Water Park near the southern end of the lake, whence she was rescued by the National Trust in 1978.

After being fitted with flotation chambers she was towed to Pier Cottage slipway, lifted from the water, and surveyed, after which in sections she was transported to Vickers' Works in Barrow for rebuilding the hull and superstructure. Locomotive Enterprises of Gateshead built a new boiler and engine.

The new all-welded hull, which incorporated parts of the original, was transported by road from Barrow in sections once again for assembly on the same Pier Cottage slipway which had seen the building of the first vessel. On 25th March 1980, the rebuilt *Gondola* returned to the lake along the same rails laid in 1859 for the original launching. Commissioned on 24th June 1980, this lovely steamer sails daily throughout the summer. The elegant lines of this charming vessel give present-day tourists a nostalgic glimpse of Victorian splendour, enabling them to share an experience of which, among others, Arthur Ransome, Thomas Carlyle and John Ruskin wrote with evident admiration and affection.

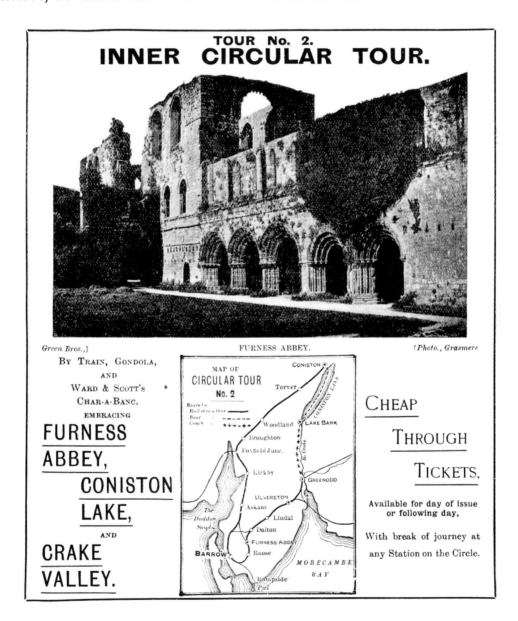

Tour advertisement 1907. Taken from a booklet given free to potential travellers to advertise the tours run by the Furness Railway. The Inner Circular tour allowed passengers to travel round the south-west corner of the Lake District by rail, coach and steamer.

(Geoff Holme collection)

Crews of Gondola *and* Lady of the Lake, *c.1910. The captains of the two vessels pose together with their crews. Captain Hamill, seated centre left, was captain of Gondola while Captain Priss, seated centre right, was captain of Lady of the Lake.*

(Barbara Priss, Ken Norman collection)

Captain Priss on Gondola. *Dressed up for inclement weather, Captain Priss is at the helm of Gondola. The modern vessel now has a cockpit with railings round for protection of the crew.* *(Barbara Priss, Ken Norman collection)*

Lake Bank pier. *Captain Priss is seen waiting for his next turn of duty at Lake Bank pier.*

(Barbara Priss, Ken Norman collection)

Of the many people who still remember the Coniston line, the doyen is surely Major John Hext of Holywath. He used the railway from boyhood, and has memories of the line going back to the 1920s.

He remembers, with little pleasure, travelling to the dentist in Barrow, and, in a much happier frame of mind, coming home for school holidays. He can remember the old Furness 6-wheel carriages being painted in their final all-over blue livery, and being hauled by the 'brick red' locomotives provided by the Furness. His favourite locomotives from this era were the short lived 4-4-2 tank engines built to replace the earlier small tanks. The guard, Willy Reddon, was a great friend who sometimes allowed him to travel in the brake van. Willy was the guard right up to the introduction of the 'Motor Trains', and then, at the age of 63 was transferred for the remaining years of his railway service to Manchester, working mainly on overnight parcel services.

The line terminated at the Copper House a few hundred yards above Coniston station, and just above Major Hext's house. Here the crushed ore was brought down from the mines by horse and cart, and sent down chutes into the wagons. The original Copper House no longer exists, but some more recent buildings on the site are now in use as a stone workshop, while, at one side of the line, pieces of shaped slate may still be found.

The piece of line between the station and the Copper House served a number of purposes. Coaches from excursion trains would be backed up on to it while the engine was prepared for the return trip. Near the end of the line were gates, on top of the bridge over the Mealy Gill, which shut off the Copper House from the rest of the line. At holiday times it was necessary to open these to fit in all the stock. The line was also used for a number of camping coaches, which were popular between the wars, with some remaining until 1957. Major Hext explained how the early morning train from Foxfield to Coniston was pushed rather than pulled up to Coniston during the summer months. This was so that the engine did not need to run past the camping coaches and disturb the residents!

Major Hext remembers, when travelling to catch the sleeper train to London, using the line from the Copper House to the station as a 'short cut' from his home. Then you could catch the 6.39 pm train, change at Foxfield and Barrow and take the sleeper train to London, arriving early next morning. Mr. Hext's family often had perishable goods sent up from London. The 10.40 am from Euston would receive a package from, say, Harrods, and could be met in good time for an evening function on the 6.30 pm arrival at Coniston. On one occasion, Mr. Hext even had his family car sent back to Coniston by train, and had to construct a special ramp to unload it!

The trains must have had a reputation for good timekeeping. The morning passenger train came in at 9.20 am and was ready to leave again at 11.00 am. It would whistle at the two crossings just south of Coniston. You could set your watch by that, said Major Hext.

The first crossing down the line was at Park Gate, which was looked after by the redoubtable Mrs Troughton. Some of the many climbers and walkers who came to Coniston would stay with Mrs Harris next to the Park Gate crossing. Engine drivers would slow on approaching the crossing, and rucksacks would be thrown from the train so that the walkers were not obliged to carry them back from the station!

Workers at the Barrow shipyard would take the 6.00 am train, and the line also provided a useful service to Barrow and Ulverston markets. A special cattle dock was constructed at Coniston station for stock in transit to market. During World War II, the line became a vital link to the outside world. Shops depended on the line for supplies, and bread came from the Co-op bakery in Barrow, unwrapped, in wooden slatted boxes.

Freight trains usually ran on three days a week, and were operated by drivers from Barrow. The slate quarries above the line depended on it and provided much of its volume of traffic in the early 20th century. Much of the slate went for roofing, until fashions changed. There was a slate wharf at Coniston station where most of the slate was handled. Slate from the Mandall's 'Blue Quarries' was loaded at the Copper House wharf, where a young John

Presentation to Harold Stephenson, Station Master, 1952. On the occasion of his promotion to Station Master at Corkickle, Whitehaven, surrounded by friends and colleagues past and present, Harold Stephenson (left) is presented with a clock by Major John Hext (right).
(John Hext collection)

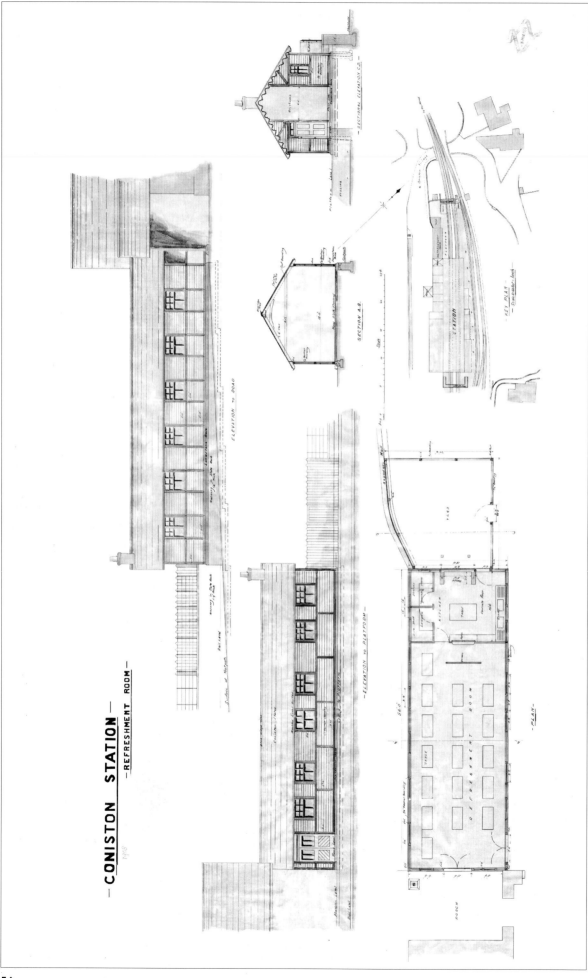

Coniston Station refreshment room. *The plan prepared by the Furness Railway drawing office for the refreshment room provided at the northern end of platform 1. Costing £376, the facility was completed and ready for use on 17th June 1905.*

(John Hext collection)

Coniston station garden, c.1958. A number of people, when talking about their memories of the branch, have described the railway models in the station garden. Here these models are seen amongst the plants and other features of the garden. (Ken Hodgson, Geoff Holme collection)

Hext would ride the footplate when wagons were being delivered or collected. He remembers his mother being very upset when plans were drawn up for an aerial ropeway from the slate quarries to the Copper House in case it could be seen from the house. It would have ended just outside the gate to the Copper House where, for some reason unknown to Major Hext, the LMSR had retained parts of two small fields beside the railway. Other freight carried included flour, granite, coal and building materials. The last freight train on the line carried coal for Nick Fell, the local merchant.

Perhaps the best remembered is the timber trade. This was the most prolific in the area in World War I. The local word for moving timber was snigging or sniggering. In Coniston, timber was sniggered to the station by horse teams. The road was steep and wound between walls and cottages below the station. Two teams were required and it was quite an art to guide the long loads skilfully between the obstacles. A four-ton crane was erected at the station to load the tree trunks on the long low wagons.

The mail arrived on the 7.00 am train and was despatched on the 6.39 pm train. The outgoing mail was transferred to the Travelling Post Office at Barrow, but was only postmarked 'Whitehaven to Preston TPO' on Sunday evenings, when local post offices were closed. The newspapers were collected in like manner by the local newsagent. After sorting at the station they were transported on a hand cart down to his shop in the village.

While the line was in existence, it was a local employer as well as an attraction. Staff at Coniston comprised a station master, two drivers, two firemen, six platelayers, two porters, a signalman and a porter/signalman. There was also a night cleaner who was supposed to keep the fire burning in the engine during the night. If the first train of the morning was late, it was probably because the cleaner had fallen asleep and there was no steam!

Mr Edward Woolgar was Station Master at Coniston from 1888 until he moved to Ulverston in 1902. On his retirement he settled in Coniston, becoming a County Alderman, a Magistrate, and Curator of the Coniston Museum. A staunch Liberal, he was anxious to find out as quickly as he could the result of a General Election. He instructed the driver of the branch train to find out and to let him know by whistle the result. He was delighted when the driver whistled three times at Park Gate crossing to signal a Liberal victory in the constituency.

Mr Woolgar was proud of his association with the Ruskins at Brantwood. He frequently met John Ruskin off the train at Coniston station. Returning to Coniston from Seascale on what was to be his last journey in 1889, John Ruskin said to him, 'I've returned earlier than I anticipated, but I wanted to be home again. There's no place like Coniston.'

Another who often came into contact with Ruskin was the skipper of the *Gondola*, Capt. Hamill. The travel writer W T Palmer records how Capt. Hamill told him that:

> Mr Ruskin did not like scrow [upset], I remember, and every year the [Severn] family used to go down to Lake Bank Hotel till spring cleaning was over. Mr Ruskin went with them, of course. Mr Severn used to hire the *Gondola*, and we ran in to the landing-stage to take servants and luggage on board. Now you know Mr Ruskin did not like our boat at all, … but I remember once (it was in the seventies) when we drew it to the stage, that Mr Ruskin stood there with Mrs Severn and the family. I was surprised and some pleased, I can tell you, when he came on board. He went all over the boat, into every corner while we were steaming down, looked at the engines a long while and asked a lot of sharp questions about them — he knew a fair bit about machinery in spite of his old-fashioned ways and idea. Then when we were nearing Lake Bank he came out of the saloon there, and as he passed me, said with a nice smile, 'I may like steam after all'.

After the summer services were over and *Gondola* laid up for the winter months, Capt. Hamill would work as a cleaner in the engine shed at Coniston. A fellow cleaner,

Mr J C Jackson, thought highly of his mate: *He was very agile and extremely thorough in all he did, a very reliable and good man.*

At this time there were two engines stabled at Coniston, which had two sets of men, and occasionally a cleaner would be called out for a firing turn. Mr Jackson fired for driver Jack Robinson ('Gentleman Jack'), whose liking for speed was well-known; he could cover the distance from Foxfield to Coniston, just under ten miles, in less than fifteen minutes, and this included twice reducing speed in order to exchange the tablet. He well deserved his other sobriquet of 'Hell-Fire Jack'!

In more recent times, Philip Johnstone recalls working as night cleaner at Coniston in the winter of 1956-7. One cleaner from Barrow shed would work Monday, Wednesday and Friday nights at Coniston and a second Tuesday and Thursday. Leaving Barrow on the 6.02 pm, connection was made on to the last branch train at Foxfield. The branch engine was usually Ivatt 2-6-2T 41217, *a lovely little engine.* The cleaners appreciated the rocking grate and self-cleaning smokebox. The fire was cleaned over the small ashpit, then the engine turned and berthed in the shed with the bunker sticking out opposite the coaling platform. The water tank was filled from a small tap in the shed fitted with a hosepipe; this often took until 4.30 am! Coaling was usually completed by midnight, after which it was only necessary to observe the fire, the boiler water level and the steam pressure. Anyone who has spent a night alone with a steam engine will know what strange noises they can make. It was good to hear the early-turn fireman's motorbike coming along the road at half-past four in the morning. Working three nights at Coniston, two at Barrow shed and being the Saturday night knocker-up produced a wage packet of about £13, which compared well with the £10 per week earned by the average Barrow driver.

The branch line developed an independence all of its own. By way of illustration, Driver Tom Hodgson was on the footplate of the engine in charge of the last down train. It was on the night of 5th September 1950, and there had been some four inches of rain in a short period of time. When he reached Torver, it was to find the bridge under water, and a message from Barrow Control instructing him not to proceed. Driver Hodgson was made of sterner stuff. He is reported to have said, 'Bugger Control, I'se ga-in yam' [I'm going home]. Ignoring instructions, he took the train over the bridge at Torver Beck, although unable to see the rails, and delivered his passengers safely to Coniston, where they found the Forge Bridge demolished and water pouring through the Black Bull Hotel in the worst floods of living memory.

When the Coniston line was in operation, the large station site above the village commanded a grand view to Coniston Water in one direction and to Yewdale in the other. With its splendid Victorian buildings, signal box, turntable and extensive sidings, the station itself was one of the sights of the Lake District. The station clock was double-faced, one on the platform and one in the office. There were few advertisements, but the LMS added a large, beautifully painted signboard near the exit, describing walks around Coniston and other local features. In the days before World War I, the tea rooms offered afternoon tea at 6d. or 1s. and full meals at 1s.6d., a not inconsiderable sum in those days. Many people who remember the line also remember the garden 'railway' on part of the site where the tearoom once stood.

The number of people who remember the line even in its latter years is now diminishing. However, by writers, photographers and others who do remember the line sharing their memories with the younger generation, the branch will continue to live on for many years to come.

End of the line, c.1946. The end of the branch by the bridge over Mealy Gill. The gate across the line here defined the limit of maintenance by the railway company and was kept locked. A block placed on the rail prevented unsecured vehicles in the Copper House running down the line to the station. Major Hext remembers taking this photo together with two others shortly after his return from active service during World War II. (John Hext)

lifting had finished the previous day ran his train off the end of the remaining track while reading his newspaper.

Nothing that could be of further use to the railway was left behind, and even the platform coping stones were removed. The footbridge at Coniston was dismantled, and the span was later re-erected by the Ravenglass and Eskdale Railway at Ravenglass. At the time of writing it has been removed due to station layout improvements and is in store pending a re-use elsewhere on the railway. The signal box was demolished before the rest of the buildings, and the frame removed. A 24-lever portion of it was re-used to replace the original frame at Park South when that was worn out, where it still remains in use.

The land was sold off piecemeal, mainly to farmers whose land it dissected. This process started shortly after the branch was lifted around 1965, and has resulted in parts being ploughed back into the fields. In other places one fence was simply removed. Some of these fences are still in use today and can be made out by their typical railway appearance. Parts of the track bed were used as a route for the new water main to serve High Furness from Levers Water constructed in 1974. This included part of the route from the Copper House to where an electricity substation blocked the route just north of Coniston station, and also part of the route north of Torver.

Other parts of the track bed, notably north of Broughton and on the approach to Park Gate Crossing, are now open to the public as footpaths, although unfortunately it has not been possible to open the full length of the branch for the public to enjoy. The stretch from Dalton Road crossing (south of Torver) to Torver station has been used for road improvements.

Many of the bridges have been removed over the years. The bridge south of Torver station and the one south of Park Gate crossing both succumbed to road improvements. The largest structure on the branch known as 'Five Arches', between Broughton and Woodland, was simply too expensive to maintain once no longer required for the railway, and to save ongoing costs was demolished. The bridge at the north end of Coniston station also suffered this fate. A few bridges are still in use for other purposes, as with the structure over Mealy Gill adjacent to the Copper House which now carries the 1974-built water main from the fells. Others still serve their original purpose, providing access between fields dissected when the railway was built.

The station buildings at Torver, Woodland and Broughton were sold off as private houses and remain in domestic use. The crossing cottages at Dalton Road and Bush Green also remain as private houses.

In April 1965 the North Western Evening Mail reported:

> Mystery surrounds the future of Coniston's disused railway station ...The building has stood derelict for three years since the lines were torn up. ... The once pretty rail terminal overlooking Coniston Water has fallen into wrack and ruin. It is strewn with rubbish and overgrown with weeds, vandals have smashed pane upon pane of glass, doors hang loosely on their hinges and the slate roof is in a terrible state of disrepair.

This state of affairs lingered on until December 1968 when, ten years after its closure, the Roads Department of North Lonsdale Rural Council pulled the station down. The site is now occupied by light industrial units and housing,

Coniston station, c.1963. After the track was lifted, the station site remained derelict, with only the station name board surviving to indicate the building had been a station. The signal box has been demolished to allow recovery of the frame for re-use elsewhere. The name board survived and is now on display at the Ruskin Museum in the village. (Michael Andrews MAA 129)

and a keen eye is needed to find the few reminders that there was once a busy station at this site.

Railways still continue at Coniston with a private 7¼in-gauge railway constructed by John Hext in the grounds of his home at Holywath. This includes a number of items he purchased from British Railways when they lifted the branch in 1963/1964. The branch line is also remembered by the many modellers who reproduce this attractive line in smaller gauges.

As the years pass, while the trains have gone and the railway lifted, the Coniston Railway will live on in the memories of those who knew and used it. Others must be content to let their imagination be stimulated by the many portraits, in word and image, this lovely little line has inspired over the years. And *Gondola*, in all its splendour, still plies on Coniston Water, nearly 150 years after James Ramsden knocked away those wedges.

Holywath Railway, *c.1977. Happily a number of items were saved when the branch was demolished, and the former ground frame cabin from the north end of the station is seen here in the grounds of Holywath, at Coniston. The owner, Major John Hext, is seen with one of the locomotives used on his railway. In the foreground is a former signal of LNWR design recovered from the station site.* (John Hext collection)

The end, *c.1963. Framed by the bridge west of Park Gate Crossing carrying the main A593 road from Torver into the village, the demolition train works its way down the branch towards Torver. The bridge has since been demolished to allow road improvements on what was a difficult and narrow bend.* (Michael Andrews MAA 131.1)

In 1957 British Railways carried out a survey of passenger traffic on the Coniston branch. This showed that, on weekdays in winter, an average of 18 passengers joined each of the sixteen trips per day (8 round trips) run by the motor train. This low figure reflects the fact that there was a long-established Ribble Motors bus service between Ulverston and Coniston (originally started by J Creighton around 1926), with 6 round trips each weekday, taking 54 minutes for the journey, and connecting with the Barrow Corporation / Ribble Joint Service between Ulverston and Barrow. Closure of the Coniston Branch passenger service was estimated to save some £17,000 per annum. In spite of protests by local authorities, Friends of the Lake District and numerous individuals, closure was approved. It took place on 6th October 1958, after being delayed from the original scheduled date of 15th September 1958 due to local objections. Ironically closure took place just before the new secondary school opened at Coniston which drew in pupils from a large area including that served by the branch.

The last passenger train to use the branch arrived at the station at 9.20 pm on Saturday, 4th October 1958. Mr T Watson drove the train into Coniston, with Mr Ron

Closure Notice, 1961. Complete closure of the branch took place on 30th April 1962 after the statutory procedures initiated by this notice had taken place. (Michael Andrews MAA 133)

Gaitskell as his fireman. A relief crew returned the train to Barrow for the last time. It was an occasion of great nostalgia and loss to the community. Closure had been made conditional on the provision of a replacement bus service. This was provided by Ribble Motors from their Ambleside depot, who retained two 7 ft 6 in wide 35-seaters until road improvements were carried out. These were TS7s of 1936 vintage, re-bodied and fitted with 7.4 litre diesel engines. For noise, vibration and rough riding, they beat the old railmotor hands down. They were also found very inconvenient when loading the mailbags they were obliged to carry. Often, an 8 ft-wide vehicle was used. These rode much better, but there were problems when meeting oncoming traffic on the narrow road. On at least one occasion the conductor had to open a gate into a field for the driver to 'park' his bus to let the traffic pass.

Inevitably, punctuality was not good and connecting trains at Foxfield were sometimes missed. As a consequence the service was not popular despite the expensive road improvements. When in 1961 the road collapsed under the school bus local mothers demanded 'Bring back the passenger trains'. It was a call which fell on deaf ears.

British Railways paid Ribble Motors £5000 per annum to operate the service but fares amounted only to some £2000 per annum. By the winter of 1963-4, the service had reduced to 6 weekday buses taking 34 minutes each way, which were increased to 8 each way for the following summer. This compared with 7 weekday buses from Ulverston to Coniston and 8 in the return direction, each taking 54 minutes, with one additional service in summer.

Apart from a 'school bus' leaving Foxfield at 8.45 am and returning from Coniston at 3.50 pm (still running today), the replacement service was discontinued in October 1968. In recent years Asda Supermarket at Barrow has started to run a free bus service for customers from Coniston via Broughton. At the time of writing the winter bus service between Ulverston and Coniston has improved to 8 daytime services from Ulverston to Coniston and 10 in the return direction during school term, although none now run after teatime, isolating the village for all but car owners.

An 'enthusiast special' used the line on 27th August 1961, when Fowler 4F 0-6-0 No. 44347 hauled this final passenger train to Coniston and back to Foxfield as part of the Furness Railtour. Originating in Manchester, this was jointly organised by the Stephenson Locomotive Society and the Manchester Locomotive Society, and earlier in the day the train had visited other Furness branch lines long since closed to passengers.

The freight service on the branch was discontinued on 30th April 1962. The lifting of the permanent way using a demolition train with a steam crane began soon after the freight closure, starting with the line to the Copper House and the station area trackwork. Ironically, diesels which never normally worked on the branch were to be the normal traction power for these demolition trains, with Metropolitan Vickers type 2 Co-Bo diesels, by then all based at Barrow, being used. It is reputed that, on one occasion, the driver of the locomotive propelling the train to where

Demolition train at Coniston, *1963. Demolition of the branch followed shortly after closure, with most of the work being carried out during 1963 by the railway's own staff based at Barrow. Here a Metro-Vic Co-Bo locomotive is heading the scrap train and ready for lifting the track in the train shed, the rails serving platform 3 having already been recovered. Nothing re-usable was left behind, the frame from the signal box being re-used at Park South near Barrow where it is still in operation, while the footbridge was installed on the Ravenglass and Eskdale Railway at Ravenglass.* (Philip Johnstone)

Demolition, *c.1963. Here the demolition crane prepares to dismantle the next panel and lift the track components onto the wagons behind for transport back to Barrow.* (Michael Andrews MAA 128)

ACKNOWLEDGMENTS

The authors wish to thank the following for providing assistance with the research for this book:

The Clerk of the Records, House of Lords Record Office for Parliamentary Acts, bills, deposited plans and proceedings of committees on bills.

The Keeper of the Records, Public Record Office, Kew for the records of the Furness Railway Company and of the Board of Trade Railway Department.

The Director of the British Library for maps and plans and files of local newspapers.

Area Archivist, Barrow Record Office for use of the local collection including the Kendall Collection, plans deposited by the former Civil Engineer, British Rail, Preston and the microfilm copy of the Diary of the 7th Duke of Devonshire.

The authors have received considerable help from John Hext of Coniston who had observed and used the Coniston branch since early LMSR days. His reminiscences have made a considerable contribution to the book and in particular to Chapter 9.

Jonathan Miller of Appleby has kindly lent the authors his copy of 'The Coniston Branch Railway – Past, Present and Future' by Emma Miller and Ian Lillington, 1983, which has provided useful data. The paper by D Butterworth, 'Coniston Branch, Furness Railway, 1859 - 1962' (1978) has proved useful.

Over many years a number of individuals have given the authors assistance with this project. While it is not possible to name them all, thanks must go to Mike Faulkner for his work in preparing many of the drawings used in the book from the original Furness Railway plans or, where buildings survive, by survey.

In more recent times Alan Johnstone has used his computing skills to draw maps and redraw the plans ready for publication, and to set out the book for publishing. Alan Headech provided a draft text for Chapter 7, for which the authors are particularly grateful.

The authors wish to thank the many people who have loaned photographs for research or publication, and those used are acknowledged individually.

Finally, Ken Norman of Barrow, veteran writer on the Furness Railway, and Alan Pearsall, maritime and railway historian, formerly of the National Maritime Museum, have read the manuscript and made valuable suggestions. Ken Norman has also prepared the index.

Any errors or omissions are the responsibility of the authors.

REFERENCES

[1]   **T A Beck:** *Annals of Furness* (1844)

[2]   **A Cameron & E Brown:** *The Story of Coniston* (Coniston, 2002)

[3]   **P Fleming:** *Coniston Copper Mines* (Coniston, 2000)

[4]   **D Joy:** *A Regional History of the Railways of Great Britain, Volume 14, The Lake Counties* (David & Charles, 1983)

[5]   **H V Koop:** *Broughton in Furness – a History* (Beckermet, 1975)

[6]   **J D Marshall:** *Furness and the Industrial Revolution* (Barrow, 1958)

[7]   **J Melville & J L Hobbs:** *Early Railway History in Furness* (Kendal, 1951)

[8]   **K Norman:** *The Furness Railway* (Kettering, 2001)

[9]   **W T Palmer:** *The English Lakes* (London, 1905)

[10]   **H Postlethwaite:** *Cumberland Motor Services 1921-1996* (Glossop, 1996)

[11]   **J Postlethwaite:** *Mines and Mining in the English Lake District* (Whitehaven, 1913)

[12]   **J Richardson:** *Furness Past & Present* (1880)

Back Cover

Top	From an original painting by Vic Welch first published in Trains Illustrated of November 1958.	(CRA Collection)
Middle Left	Selection of Branch Line Tickets.	(Private Collection)
Middle Right	The arms of le Fleming, Lords of the Manor of Coniston.	(from Richardson's Furness Past & Present)
Bottom	The Gondola at Waterhead Pier, Coniston Lake.	(Geoff Holme collection)

Publications of the Cumbrian Railways Association are produced by the Publications Subcommittee:
Mike Peascod (Chairman), Rock Battye, Les Gilpin and Alan Johnstone.

Index